LETTERS TO Lilly

LETTERS TO Lilly

Lessons in Leadership & Loving Yourself

BY ALEXIAN WINES AND MELISSA COHEN

THIN LEAF PRESS | LOS ANGELES

Library of Congress Cataloging-in-Publication Data
Names: Wines, Alexian; Cohen, Melissa
Title: *Letters to Lilly: Lessons in Leadership & Loving Yourself*
LCCN: On File

ISBN 978-1-968318-40-6 (hardcover) | 978-1-968318-39-0 (paperback)
ISBN 978-1-968318-38-3 (eBook)

Professional Development, Leadership, Self-Help, Success

Cover Design: 100 Covers
Interior Design: Dindo Sanguenza
Editor: Dhanliza Cellona
Thin Leaf Press
Los Angeles

THIN
LEAF

Foreword

Letters to Lilly is a poignant exploration of what it means to lead with intention, integrity, and self-awareness. In this collection of letters to a younger self, Alexian "Ali" Wines and Melissa Cohen offer more than guidance as they highlight those navigating the evolving landscape of personal and professional growth. With clarity and empathy, these letters remind us that leadership is not a destination but a lifelong practice rooted in self-understanding.

Each letter unfolds as a reflection on a pivotal moment in the journey of people the world over: moments of triumph and doubt, success and struggle. Integrated within each story is a lesson in leadership and a gentle reminder to practice self-compassion. Through this unique fusion of memoir and mentorship, writers reveal a truth often overlooked: that our greatest strength as leaders comes from our willingness to know, trust, and nurture ourselves.

Letters to Lilly derives its name from an essential principle: Lessons in Leadership and Loving Yourself. This concept lies at the heart of the book and serves as an invitation to redefine leadership not as control or conquest, but as connection: to purpose, to others, and to oneself. The voices are both wise and relatable, speaking to readers at every stage of their journey with authenticity and grace.

What distinguishes this work is its elegant balance of vulnerability and vision. Ali and Melissa highlight the perspective of experience but retain the curiosity of younger selves. The result is a series of global reflections that feel both personal and universal, each letter a mirror through which readers may recognize their own aspirations, insecurities, and growth.

Letters to Lilly is not only a roadmap for emerging leaders; it is a call to approach life and work with courage, compassion, and conviction. In a world that often measures success by speed and status, Ali and Melissa re-center the conversation on mindfulness, empathy, and the enduring power of self-belief. Each writer shares insights that remind us that leadership, at its core, begins within and that when we choose to lead ourselves with kindness, we empower others to do the same.

Enjoy!

Scott MacGregor
Publisher & EIC, Outlier Magazine
Founder, The Outlier Project
Founder & CEO, Something New, LLC

Dear *Letters to Lilly* Readers,

We are grateful that you have decided to embark on this journey with us. The concept of *Letters to Lilly (Lessons in Leadership & Loving Yourself)* was born after Alexian was diagnosed with a hole in her heart, realizing that tomorrow was not guaranteed to anyone.

With this new reality, she felt called to share some of her biggest life lessons. She strongly believes there is an urgent need for people around the world to prioritize self-love and begin to change the face of global leadership by ensuring leadership begins with heart. Many of her leadership and life lessons were not taught in the classroom; rather, they are a culmination of her life's journey to date, with her greatest growth coming from the moments in her life when she realized she was not alone.

When Ali shared her vision with Melissa, she was instantly captivated by the idea and the impact it could have on a broader scale. What started out as sharing their own personal letters, and then the letters of others, on LinkedIn is now taking its next big step: this book.

We are overwhelmed by the enthusiasm and heartfelt honesty that has come from the people who have participated in the creation of this book, which is an integral part of the *Letters to Lilly* movement.

These letters to our younger selves have come from across the globe, from writers of all walks of life. The common thread throughout is that each of us faces challenges, struggles, and hidden opportunities regardless of where we sit in the world.

The message that we hope each one of you takes away is that we are all interconnected and never truly alone in what we are experiencing. As you travel through this book, you will find letters that will make you laugh, letters that will make you cry, and letters where you will recognize yourself in the stories of others.

We are grateful to each storyteller for sharing their life lessons, experiences, hopes, and wisdom. We hope that you find their stories as inspiring as we do.

We look forward to hearing how *Letters to Lilly* has touched your heart and impacted your life.

With Love,
Ali & Melissa

Authors' note: Some writers chose to use a nickname or term of endearment when addressing their letters to Lilly.

Dear Lilly,

At this stage in your young life, as you are trying to figure out who you are and who you are meant to become, you are haunted by the words of your 8th grade English teacher. She asked you, in front of the entire class, "Does being stupid come naturally to you, or do you have to work at it?"

Her words did so much damage. She made you ask yourself, "Am I stupid?" And you assumed that if one teacher thinks you are stupid, they all must. And then there was the complete and total embarrassment that now all your classmates thought you were stupid as well. School went from a place of learning to a place where you remained silent, in fear of saying anything "stupid."

Sadly, this teacher's words will stay with you for far too long, causing you to second-guess yourself, making you afraid to speak up, and always (always) resulting in a prayer before anything public-facing that goes something like, "Please don't let me say anything stupid."

An indirect result of this is that you fall in love with the theater and movies. The ability to escape into someone else's world is like magic. Upon watching Say Anything with John Cusack, and watching his love interest, you decide to sign up for speech and debate in high school. Perhaps if you could learn to speak better, people wouldn't think you were stupid!

On the first day of class, when Mrs. G. passed out the syllabus, you immediately

panicked. "In three days, you will deliver your first speech." You looked around the room and knew there was no way you were going to be speaking in front of all of them. Nope. Not happening!

After class you visited your guidance counselor and asked to switch classes, because you couldn't speak in front of all those people. He must have agreed, because you left with a withdrawal slip to take typing. I guess he figured if you couldn't speak, you could always type.

Upon returning to the class and handing the withdrawal slip to Mrs. G to sign, the conversation didn't go quite as you'd planned:

Mrs. G: "What is this?"
You: "It's my withdrawal slip."

Mrs. G: "I can read that, but why?"
You: "I'm going to take typing."

Mrs. G: "I can read THAT, but why?"
You: "I can't speak in front of these people."

Mrs. G: "These people are your peers."
You (tears running down your face): "I can't do it."

Mrs. G (looking at you for what felt like an eternity): "And I won't do it. I won't sign this because I BELIEVE that you can do it."

Wait, what? This teacher isn't letting me out of her class? She believes in me?!

In that moment, with those seven simple words, Mrs. G changed your life. She may not have given you your voice, but she helped you find it. Above all, her belief in you begins to reverse the damage of your 8th grade teacher. One woman, seven words, life changed forever!

You stayed in the class and became one of the top speakers! You were even chosen to speak in front of members of congress (two years in a row).

Leadership Lesson:

Words Matter! Your words have power in every aspect of your life. You can do so much harm with only your words, or you can lift people with them. Use them for the good, you may just change someone's entire life! Just as there are both exceptional and awful teachers, you will find that there are also exceptional and awful leaders. A title doesn't make you a great leader. Always think about the leader that you are, or want to become. In your career, you may even need to unlearn bad behaviors you picked up from those you once thought you needed to emulate... Don't worry, it is part of the journey.

Loving Yourself Lesson:

While the belief that others have in you is empowering, nothing is more powerful than when you believe in yourself. Don't view your life through someone else's lens. Their dreams and goals are not yours, and they have never walked in your shoes. As Glinda, the Good Witch tells Dorothy, "You've always had the power my dear, you just had to learn it for yourself."

With Love,
Ali

Alexian "Ali" Wines
USA
https://linkedin.com/in/alexian-letters-to-lilly

Dear Lilly,

Some days feel exhausting and filled with angst. Believe me when I tell you, most of what you're devoting so much mental energy to is not going to matter five years from now, ten years from now... honestly, even one year from now.

This is truly a wonderful time in your life. You're young, without many of the responsibilities of adulthood weighing on you. Enjoy these years. You will look back on them fondly.

Most of all, don't think you need to have it all figured out. What your college major is doesn't have to be what your career ends up being. Your first job may end up being a lesson in what you don't want to do for the rest of your career. That's ok. That's a valuable lesson. Learn it early.

Take each experience for what it is: a lesson, an experience, and an opportunity to learn more about yourself.

It all works out in the end. Be kind to yourself and enjoy the path you're about to embark on. You're much more capable than you think. Remember that sometimes people aim to hold you back, because they will never get to where you're going.

One day you'll look back on all the things you've accomplished, and you'll smile. Trust me, I am very confident in these words.

Love,
Melissa

Melissa Cohen
USA
https://www.linkedin/com/in/melissa-beth-cohen/

Dear Lilly,

Falling down is inevitable.

You survived and thrived for a decade chasing your dreams of building a thriving business, but 2007 was a year you'll never forget.

While you chased success, you ignored your family. It wasn't intentional. Actually, you justified it by promising yourself that the hundred-hour work weeks would come to an end by the time the kids were old enough to really want you around.

But the unthinkable happened and the price was your marriage. She said you abandoned her and that was true. You were just so busy. The income was astounding, but you kept telling yourself, "Only a little while longer."

The breakup was brutal. Horrible accusations. Immense loneliness. Drinking to excess to dull the guilt and the pain.

Yet you pushed through and survived. You didn't quit even when you thought you were at the end of your life.

That prayer you said while you were laying on the kitchen floor of your condo bawling your eyes out did not fall on deaf ears.

You reframed your mind. Falling down is inevitable. Staying down is optional.

On your hands and knees, aching from the cold, ceramic tile, you stumbled over to the couch and made yourself a promise to stand up and begin moving forward. Survive this divorce and begin the march forward.

You began with getting off your own neck. Self-flagellation is unproductive and sabotages the healing process. After defeating sadness, loneliness, and self-sabotage, you forgave yourself and the healing accelerated. Thank God for the therapist!

Almost all the most powerful life lessons you learned occurred in your darkest moments and while healing, but the most important one is to make your relationships Priority #1. God, spouse, kids, family, friends…in that order.

Business will always be there to be had, and it really isn't that important by comparison to the relationships with those you love.

Redefine your relationship with the word "failure." Previously, you assigned desperately negative emotions to failing. But as a wise counselor shared with me, "ALL learning ONLY happens through failure. Almost no one 'gets it right' on the first try, and even if they do, they can't repeat the success again."

Failure doesn't become who you are. Failure is merely the achievement of a goal that is different from the one you started out trying to achieve.

Do it better or differently next time. It didn't kill you. Learn from it and move forward.

Lastly, you are resilient. Life is full of setbacks and disappointments. Don't ruminate in those, but rather zoom out, put it in perspective, extract your lessons learned… then get moving again.

Life is far too short playing to NOT LOSE. Yours is a life of abundance. Now start acting like it.

Tim Barry
USA

Dear Lilly,

The question that started it all: *"You don't have nothing to say?"*

I can still hear Dad's voice asking that question as you sat in the McDonald's booth, finishing off what was now your not-so-happy meal. At 8 years old, you were fine with being the quiet one. It meant you could observe and stay hidden. Our brother and sister spoke enough for us, and silence felt safe.

But that silence came back to bite you later, especially when you wanted to be heard and weren't, when your ideas were overlooked because you hadn't practiced using your voice.

It took years to refine that quiet observation and learn how to channel it into your voice. In time, it became your superpower...the reason you can read a room, feel energy before words are spoken, and connect dots others can't even see.

Observation taught you empathy. Listening taught you wisdom.

But in this journey to the present, somewhere deep down, something was always stirring…a voice wanting to break through the fear. College became the crucible where courage finally caught up with calling (love me some alliteration, LOL).

Every leadership role, every presentation, every unexpected "Can you speak on this?" moment pushed you out front when fear wanted to pull you back into the comfort of the background. But then those other words from Dad would bubble up: "You're a Worthey."

Our name became your Jedi Force. And in those scary moments, Dad was our Yoda…reminding us, in his own way, to push through the fear.

You didn't realize it then, but when Dad asked that fateful question: "You don't have nothing to say?" he was really calling something out of you. His pressing about your silence was his way of challenging you to use what he knew was already there.

Being a "Worthey" carried a legacy of grit and grace and represented the power to push through your fear just like Dad and his dad before us. It summoned the courage

Dad showed when he joined the Navy at 19, earned his GED, and became the first man in our family to earn a bachelor's degree. It carried the perseverance of his dad, who rose from being a sharecropper to building an asphalt business in the Deep South, all without knowing how to read.

That same power lived in you: quiet, steady, and burning beneath the surface… embers waiting for the bonfire of your voice to ignite.

What you didn't realize then was that the very thing that once terrified you, using your voice, would become the foundation for everything that followed: the international business you will build, the clients you will serve, and the women you will encourage to speak, lead, and show up fully.

Being quiet was never weakness; it was preparation. The stillness that once protected you became the soil that grew your strength.

So to the quiet little girl who used to actively watch (and still lives within me)… thank you.

Now, I'll carry the torch for both of us: speaking boldly, listening intentionally, and using the voice I once tucked away.

You would be proud of us.

Gina Worthey
USA
https://www.linkedin.com/in/gina-worthey/

Dear Lilly,

There's something I want you to know. Something I hope will stick with you throughout your lifetime. Your voice matters.

Speak up. Even when you feel unsure. Even when your stomach twists with fear. Even when you're not sure you have the words. And especially when someone else cannot speak for themselves.

I remember my first real test of this in my twenties, during an internship. I overheard an employee speaking about an adolescent client's body in a way that made my skin crawl. I felt scared, small, and completely unprepared. My voice shook as I recounted it to my supervisor, and I cried. But I shared it anyway. That moment felt terrifying, yet it taught me something I have carried ever since: courage is not the absence of fear. It's acting, and speaking, in spite of it.

Since then, I've learned that speaking up is rarely easy. Sometimes, my voice still quivers, and the fear doesn't always disappear. But I've also seen how meaningful it can be. Speaking up has opened doors, built trust, and shaped the way people see me: as someone willing to advocate for what is right.

It has allowed me to be a voice for those who cannot speak for themselves and has strengthened my own sense of integrity. Each time, I've chosen courage over comfort, I've felt the quiet, powerful ripple of doing the right thing.

Remember this: "Speak the truth even if your voice shakes." ~Maggie Kuhn.

Let it guide you. Use your voice. Protect what is right. Advocate for those without a voice. It may feel uncomfortable, scary, or even impossible at times, but the impact of your courage will be profound.

In learning to speak up, you'll discover that courage is not just a single moment. It becomes a way of living, a lens through which you approach your work, your relationships, and your life.

Lilly, embrace the fear. Let it remind you that what matters most is worth standing for. Your voice, your courage, and your choices have the power to change the world, and that is a gift you will carry with you forever.

With love and encouragement,
Melissa

Melissa Lewis-Stoner
USA
https://www.linkedin.com/in/melissalewisstoner/

Dear Lilly,

I knew you felt out of place sometimes. You were just a little girl in a small city in Southeast Asia who fell in love with languages, even though you had almost no resources to learn or practice—not even a foreigner in sight. You were the girl who carried a dictionary in her bag, dreaming of exploring the world and speaking new languages. Your dream felt too big for the space you were in. When people asked what you wanted to study and you said, "foreign languages," they looked puzzled. They couldn't see how it would lead to a job, a future, a life. You felt like an alien. But you weren't wrong. You were just early.

While no one believed in you, I couldn't say for sure that your family fully understood your choice, but I knew they didn't stop you because they loved you. You walked forward even when the path was blurry. You doubted yourself, wondered if you had chosen the right road. But you trusted your instincts. Trusted your research.

Trusted your effort. That combination—heart and mind—carried you through.

There were moments of doubt and disheartening, especially when you compared yourself to others who had more opportunities. But in your third year of university, a professor shared a story that changed your perspective. She spoke of a classmate who had lived abroad since childhood and seemed naturally gifted. But behind that success were years of isolation, struggle, and perseverance. The lesson was clear: You cannot judge someone by the moment they succeed. You must respect the journey, even if you don't know the full story. And remember, if you put in the same hours, you can get there too.

You pushed yourself hard—sometimes too hard. You believed you had to achieve everything you set your heart on, overcome every challenge life threw your way. But the truth is, life is full of trade-offs. You will not get everything. You will have to choose. And sometimes, you will fall. That's okay. Be kind to yourself. You are allowed to pause. You are allowed to lose. You are allowed to be human.

Lastly, over time, people drifted. Friends you once laughed with became names on a screen—or disappeared entirely. That wasn't anyone's fault. Time filtered people.

But when someone reaches out just because they miss you—not because they need anything—cherish them. They're rare. They're real.

You have come so far, Lilly. And you'll go even further. Keep believing. Keep learning. Keep being you.

With love,
Nichagorn

Nichagorn Ooppapong
Thailand
https://www.linkedin.com/in/nichagorn-ooppapong/

Dear Lilly,

I hope this letter finds you well. As I reflect on my 40 years of living in America, I want to share insights on leadership, self-love, and the courage to explore our calling. We live in a time when racism and stereotypes are magnified, yet you hold a powerful position to serve the person you once were. Cherish your experiences and celebrate your hard work as a Chinese American immigrant.

First, your immigrant journey is filled with challenges and opportunities. Arriving in a new country, struggling with the language, and helping with the family restaurant while pursuing education was no easy feat. The weight of expectations from family and society can be overwhelming. You learned that hard work alone does not guarantee respect or success. True leadership begins with self-acceptance and the courage to stand firm in your beliefs. Let go of the pain from past stereotypes; you are meant to inspire others who share similar experiences.

Second, Chinese culture is collective, while American culture celebrates individualism. There's so much tension between the two, and you have worked hard to balance between these two values. In a collective culture, we often prioritize others' needs, sometimes at the expense of our own well-being. Remember your early career days, working tirelessly for others, driven by a desire to please? Setting no boundaries led to burnout, especially after your father's passing, when you took on the responsibility of caring for your mother. You longed for her acceptance and praise but were often disappointed. Recognizing that your worth is not tied to others' validation, including your parents, is crucial. Embrace who you are, flaws and strengths alike. Give yourself credit, Lilly; you have come a long way.

Third, I admire your courage to trust yourself despite facing rejections. Learning to break free from people-pleasing is essential, especially in an industry that often discourages assertiveness. Saying "NO" to what doesn't serve you has opened doors to opportunities aligned with your true self. Although it may feel like a yo-yo practice, your grit shines through, and I am proud of you.

Fourth, I am most proud of you for leaping into entrepreneurship. This decision allowed you to create a life that reflects and lives your values. You understood that the grass might be greener on the other side. By building your own business, you've redefined success on your terms and fostered an environment where you can thrive without compromising your identity. Your journey of mentorship, podcasting, and authorship has empowered others. You bravely embraced falling as a stepping stone to growth, for yourself and those who join you.

Lilly, continue to embrace your journey with love and courage. Trust yourself and set boundaries, even when they may seem like unpopular choices. Leadership starts from within, and by nurturing self-love, you will inspire others to do the same.
Remember, you are enough just as you are.

With love and wisdom,
Ashley Cheung

Ashley F. Cheung
Virginia, USA

Dear Zheka,

You are six right now—curious, kind, always asking why. You like when others win. You clap the loudest when someone else shines. That is the first spark of leadership, though you don't know it yet.

One day, you'll learn that being a leader isn't about standing in front. It's about standing beside. It's about holding space when others falter, about letting them borrow your strength when they forget their own. It's a service—not a title. And sometimes, it's a sacrifice.

Leadership will break your heart a little. You'll be the one who stays up when everyone else goes home. You'll shoulder blame quietly and share credit loudly. There will be moments when no one sees the weight you carry— and those are the moments that will shape you the most.

You'll be tempted to think leaders are born or chosen. But the truth is, it's a choice you make—again and again—to care more than the world tells you to. To listen longer. To stand back so others can step forward. And, sometimes, to walk alone so others can rest.

I've lived that truth in rooms full of noise and in moments of silence. I've built things that worked and things that didn't. I've learned that the greatest power a leader has is not control—it's **belief**. Belief in people before they believe in themselves. Belief that good wins, even when it's quiet.

You will lead because you love people. You'll lead because seeing others succeed makes your heart light up. And yes, it will hurt sometimes, but it will also fill you in ways nothing else can.

When it gets hard, remember this: Leadership is love in action. It's courage wrapped in service. It's the steady hand behind every success story.

And you, my curious, funny, kind Zheka—you will be a good one. Because you already know how to see others, and that's where all true leadership begins.

With all my love,
Older "Zheka" a.k.a. Eugina

Eugina Jordan
USA
https://www.linkedin.com/in/euginajordan/

Dear Lilly,

One day you'll want to go on a life-changing adventure, and a lot of people will tell you not to do it.

You are being reckless, they'll say. You are irresponsible. You are ruining your future. Ruining your children's future. You are crazy. You are selfish.

They will recite an endless list of reasons you shouldn't, and when you try to tell them why you should, they highlight how woefully short that list is in comparison.

But what the pros and cons list will never tell you is the value of making a decision *in spite* of the risks. Because the purpose of life is to live. To live fully. To live for today, not in service of a future you cannot predict.

So even though you'll live in a lovely house, in the perfect town, with an amazing community, secure jobs and lovely school, you'll *know* that there is more to life than checking all the boxes. You'll have an itch that says, "What if?"

And so against all sound, sage and loving advice, you'll give it all up.

You'll sell the house and buy a boat, and sail around the Caribbean for two years with your husband and three young children.

You will cling desperately to the learning cliff as you try to learn all the things you need to know to stay afloat, to navigate, to fix, to teach. You will learn to accept a deep level of anxiety as you face the elements with your precious cargo down below. And you will rage at the constant breaking of things and unerring desire of this lump of fiberglass to sink.

It will be the hardest thing you will ever do. As a woman, as a mother, as a partner, and as a family.

It will also be the best.

You'll play with baby dolphins, swim in bioluminescence, do math with a mountain of conch you found on the beach. You'll spear lobster for dinner, sleep under brighter stars than you ever thought imaginable and anchor, alone, by uninhabited islands.

You'll bring a whole new meaning to working remotely. You'll watch whales breach from breakfast and build a house for hermit crabs before dinner. You'll watch your kids learn about volcanoes from climbing them, colonialism from those living its consequences, and climate change from seeing the devastation of coral reef bleaching. Those kids will learn to rewire lights, service an engine, and cook dinner because it's how you live, not what they did in school.

The pro/con list can never reconcile financial responsibility and a school curriculum with that. It's time spent together, fun made with your hands and imagination, people met, friendships made, and lessons learned.

A life well lived is not measured; it is experienced.

So, leave open the door to possibility. Remember that adventures are meant to be hard. And just because everyone else wouldn't do it, doesn't mean you shouldn't.

Tessa Rawson
Scotland
https://www.linkedin.com/in/tessarawson/

Hey There, Lilly,

Yes, you, under the duvet.

I see you trying to be still and quiet as a mouse, but you're so alert you won't get to sleep for a long time.

Even after all these years, I can still hear this "silence that is too noisy" that you wrote about. Fear that creeps in, not from the noises and shouting downstairs, but from the silence when it stops. The fear of what you're going to find when you wake up in the morning. I want to give you the strength to keep going; keep putting on this turtle-shell armor and slowly keep going. These fights were never about you, and, in time, you will need to take responsibility for your life and your choices. This year marked 45 years of their marriage, and you are grateful that they also have done their own emotional work on their lives.

The thing is, all this fear of people fighting, and fear of fathers shouting and breaking things, it actually gave you a skill of protecting yourself during the storms. Let the storm rage on *(thanks Elsa)* and when it's over, you rebuild. Rebuilding isn't too bad either, especially when you rebuild together.

You're pretty good at that as an adult now. A wife, a mother, a leader.

And this fear actually feels quite exhilarating too. You see something you're scared of, and you look it in the eye. You make a plan, work out how you can develop the skills, and then you do it. Learning how to swim as an adult was hard, but you did it. Learning how to sit in a 1:1 meeting with a male colleague whose aggressive manner triggers you into behaving like the little girl hiding under the duvet, that took time. And no one has a training course for that one.

Surround yourself with good men and women. The ones that make you feel safe, and you don't have to freeze around. Oh, and there are lots out there! Throughout earning your engineering degree, or your DJ-ing where you'd often be the only female in the room, there were many who belittle, oppress, and dominate. But also, there were plenty of men who were awesome, inspiring, and loving. They were funny, caring, supportive, and not at all aggressive or controlling. Keep these ones close. They genuinely think you're a great human.

And with the men and women who oppress and dominate in the workplace, well, they need your love too. Don't give your love endlessly, but give your love patiently and intentionally to help them grow. This patriarchy hurts them too.

So dear Lanko-Polanko, with your massive glasses...

Please just keep smiling, keep your humor, and keep standing up for yourself.

Love from,

Your future big adult self, who is currently writing this snuggled under my duvet with a cup of tea, next to a hilarious and brave little 6-year-old girl, and a deeply loving husband.

Fabia Jeddere-Fisher
United Kingdon
https://www.linkedin.com/in/fabia-jeddere-fisher-b6911632/

Dear Young Carlos,

There is so much I'd like to tell you, and I don't want to prevent you from learning from your own experience, but I will say this:

It's been a long time since I was able to think like a child; I miss it.

I know that you wish you were older so you could get respect. But let me break it to you: That's a very lofty goal—for earning respect can take a very long time.

There will be few people genuinely interested in what you have to say, who will support you and care about you. Not even your first or perhaps second wife might fully respect you, so you better be careful who you marry. Pay attention to the red flags. Longevity in a relationship comes not from attraction or commonality but rather from admiration and appreciation of your differences, your ability to respect each other's thoughts, and being able to make compromises. Those compromises can be on everything, from daily mundane things to critical things like raising a family and caring for the other when they're not having a good day or when they are ill.

There may be times when you feel like you don't fit in. That's a good thing; you don't need to fit in, so don't fight it. We need critical thinkers who view things from different perspectives. And if it feels like where you live is not where you can thrive, consider leaving, to another city or even another country. Don't take what doesn't fit you. But know that it's going to be hard, particularly if you move somewhere with a different culture and language. Even worse, one where most people have a skin color lighter than yours.

Be prepared to run faster than everyone else. Everything will be hard; you'll be judged by your background. Your good qualities will go unnoticed, it will be hard to be heard, respected, or given the opportunity to grow.

Follow your instincts and your heart, but also use your brain to apply logic, and learn to communicate well. Communication is everything; your best ideas and qualifications are nothing if you can't articulate them. You need to convince them first.

And if you do learn to be noticed, to communicate, to articulate, and to be trusted; and if you're lucky enough to have earned the privilege of being in a leadership position, please never forget that you're working with humans. Never forget where you came from: build your team, believe in them, make them successful, because their success will mean your success.

Now here is the thing; if you're able to do all that, you will finally receive the respect you've been dreaming of for the entirety of your life. From the people you've built, and from the people who now look up to you for your tenacity, your resilience, and for all your contributions that helped make this world a better place, one thought and one idea at a time...

Carlos Abrego
Canada
https://www.linkedin.com/in/cafecarlos/

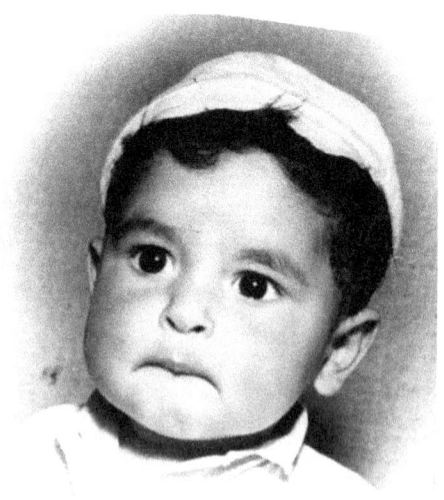

Dear Lilly,

It's been more than two decades since I met you in the gift shop. We were in line at the check-out when you turned and said, "My name is Lilly!"

I said, "Well hello, Lilly. How are you?"

Pressing your small hand against your cheek, you whispered,

> "Daddy and me are shopping
> for Mommy's birthday!"

Your parents, who were standing next to you, both grinned at your 'secret' announcement. It was obvious the ginger-haired man was your father. The curly locks that touched your shoulders were the same shade of red. Your hair and the lilt in your voice brought to mind images of the Scottish Highlands. Sweeping the sides of your skirt in a churning motion, you looked up at me and asked,

"Have you seen Frozen?"

I had to admit that I hadn't, and asked, "Have you?"

"Oh yes! SEVEN times!"

The expression on my face must have been of disbelief because your father smiled and said,

"Yes, it's true. We bought the movie for her."

You continued, "I just LOVE Elsa! I know you'd love her too!"

Your gifts were bagged, and you followed your parents to the exit. Skipping behind and waving, you sang out,

"Bye-bye-eee!"

I waved back and watched as your father open a car door and you hopped in.

"Ten fifty-nine please Ma'am."

…"Ma'am, that will be ten fifty-nine," the clerk repeated, bringing me back to the present.

How I wanted to stay in the moment where you were, to hear more of your stories, your thoughts and feelings. I was inspired by your vitality, joy, and openness. Had you been a childhood friend of mine, I believe you would have accepted me as I was, though it would have been hard for me to understand. You see, strangers often turned away from me, and I wasn't readily included in my elementary school circles. But you were different; you seemed to want to connect with me. I expect you haven't changed, and that you've grown into a most amiable young woman with a plethora of close friends.

Had we been of the same vintage and known each other, I'm certain we would have been the best of companions. I like to imagine we might even have been related— cousins, perhaps. We shared a common trait, although my shade of red hair was much darker than yours. Still, we definitely would have bonded. When we played together, I would have shown you my collections of sea shells and book of drawings.

We would have regular playdates, and on Sundays when my grandpa came to visit, I'd call you to come over. You'd join me in laughing at our reflections in his 1947 highly polished black Pontiac sedan. We'd move back and forth, churning the folds of our full skirts and giggling as our body shapes turned from plump and wide to tall, pencil thin impressions on the car's gleaming contours. You'd be enthusiastic and full of joy, just as you were in the gift shop. You'd be open and accepting, completely oblivious to the purple birthmark that covered my right cheek, a lifelong scourge that prevented me from being me.

Corinne

Corinne Cowan
Alberta, Canada
https://www.linkedin.com/in/corinne-cowan

Dear Lilly,

Have you ever looked around and thought, *"Dang. This isn't where I thought I'd be."*

Sometimes that realization comes quietly. A whisper that something's off.
Other times, it festers like a sliver you keep trying to ignore.
And then there are the moments that hit hard, when you walk straight into the truth that something has to change.

I've had a few of those over my growth journey. I acted swiftly, and people around me called it brave or courageous. I couldn't connect to that description until much later, when I realized courage doesn't always feel like strength in the moment. Sometimes it feels like loss. Like uncertainty. Like standing in the in-between. Not who you were or where you were, not yet who you'll be or where you're going.

That space can feel disorienting, but it's also where something honest begins to surface—where the noise quiets just enough for you to hear what's real.

Over the years, I've learned that self-love is leadership, and both begin there.
It's not failure. It's an invitation.

Leadership, I've learned, isn't about getting louder or stronger.
It's about permission. The permission to soften into awareness, to notice where you tighten, where you shrink, and where something new is quietly asking for space.

The most courageous leaders I know aren't the ones who always know the next move.
They're the ones who pause long enough to listen to the story underneath their striving.
They honor endings before rushing toward beginnings.

So, Lilly, when you find yourself in that in-between, when the old patterns don't quite fit and the new ones haven't formed, don't rush to fill the silence.
That's where wisdom grows.
That's where you learn to lead yourself.

The noisy world will try to hand you scripts about success, strength, and certainty.
But your leadership and your peace will live in your ability to write your own.

Toss the script.
Hold the pen.

With warmth and light,
Jackie J

Jackie Johnston
United States
https://www.linkedin.com/in/jackie-jj/

Dear Lilly,

I was born into a very modest family, where dreams often had to wait their turn behind daily realities. Life wasn't easy, but even as a child, I believed there was one thing that could change everything: EDUCATION. Books became my doorway to possibility, my way of rewriting my family's story.

Step by step, I found my way into the world of human resources. It wasn't a straight path; there were late nights, missed moments, and many quiet battles. But I kept moving forward, guided by leaders who believed in me and by the quiet voice inside that said, "Keep going."

But not every leader I met could truly see me. They measured my worth against their idea of what success should look like, and in their gaze, my contributions often felt small. I came to understand that discrimination doesn't always arrive in loud, obvious ways. Sometimes it hides behind polite smiles, behind compliments that sting, behind doors that quietly close. It moves softly, but it leaves deep marks. There were moments I wanted to give up, moments when the challenges seemed endless.

Then came the pandemic. The world changed overnight. Businesses closed, people lost their jobs, and I was not spared. Suddenly, I found myself in the middle of a financial crisis, struggling to hold things together while my family faced one health battle after another. Cancer crept into our lives, again and again, and each time, it felt like the storm was getting stronger.

Just when I felt the weight was too heavy to carry, an angel entered my life, my leader, my mentor, my inspiration. "SHE" taught me what it meant to be brave. She reminded me that no matter how dark the days are, there's always light ahead. Every time I doubted myself, she stood beside me, unwavering. I learned to lift my chin, breathe deeply, and whisper to myself, "A brighter day is just one step away." That became my mantra, a promise I made to myself to keep walking, even when the path disappears. I learned that when life pushes you down, you must push yourself even harder to rise, not just for yourself, but for those who look to you for light.

And when you trust yourself and trust the universe, somehow, life begins to flow again. The right people, the right moments, and the right opportunities start to find their way back to you.

So, dear Lilly, if you ever feel that the world is testing you beyond your limits, remember this:

You are stronger than every challenge you face. You are braver than every doubt that whispers against you. And you are exactly where you need to be to begin again.

Keep believing! Keep rising!
The universe has a way of rewarding those who refuse to give up.

With gratitude and warmth,
Tasha

Thatcheenee (Tasha) Munusamy
Malaysia
https://www.linkedin.com/in/thatcheenee-munusamy-a5862b60/

Dear Sally Joy,

There is so much I want to tell you! And also, so much you need to learn on your own because, as I know you'll come to see one day, the most important life lessons don't happen in traditional classrooms, not even for teacher's pet, perfect-attendance, straight-A kind of folks who love control like you do.

Because here's one thing I will share without giving too much away: Life tosses everyone wildcards. Yes, even you.

Before you panic, I can tell you your hard work will get you to many destinations you dream of—which, deep breath, will include Harvard and Stanford, along with companies you don't even know yet! Life will still hand you challenges.

Moments when things don't go according to plan.
Experiences that feel far from "perfect."
Things you think will break you.

Except they won't.
They'll reveal you.

Your biggest challenges will uncover an inner strength you can't yet imagine, a resilience others already see but you can't. Because to see it, something must not work out. And in all the pressure you put on yourself to be perfect, you're missing out on this: permission to be human.

So I'm giving you that now, even though I know it'll be hard to trust me. But I hope you do.

Because despite what you think now, the best moments in life have something better than perfection: connection. And over time, you'll learn that being vulnerable and letting others truly know all of you isn't weakness. In fact, it will become your greatest strength.

And speaking of strengths, it turns out everyone has them. They're just not all the same. There are many ways to be gifted, and not all of them involve doing well at school or getting advanced degrees.

And even though you'll earn yours, you'll find your way by trusting your heart more than your head. Yes, you're a brilliant classroom student, but you're also a beautiful student of life. You'll learn to say yes to what feels right, not just what looks right. And one day, people all over the world will be moved by your words: your heartfelt, heart-strong, rainbow-after-the-storm words that authentically help others see silver linings.

Because they reveal your capacity to see them for yourself too.

But I promise all of that will come in time. For now, I hope you can stress less and smile more. Like you did when you were little, before grades and reviews and other people's opinions weighed you down.

And as you do, you'll find and create joy every chance you get.

Just like Mom and Dad hoped when they gave you your middle name.

A name you didn't initially like but grow to love, embody, and work to bring into the world daily. Because unlike the A's you earned for yourself, joy is something you'll share with everyone.

Love always,
Me

P.S. Be nicer to your sister. She's wiser than you realize.

Sally Joy Wolf
USA
https://www.linkedin.com/in/sally-wolf-932139/

Dear Lilly,

You never really fit in. I know it. You know it.

What did we expect? We are the eternal contradiction. British Nigerian—or Nigerian British? Extroverted introvert. Comfortable in solitude yet thriving in a career built on connection.

Think back to when we were eight and the early years that shaped us:

The smoky aroma of roasted corn in the streets of Lagos.

Your manic squeals with your brothers when you found a scorpion in Jos.

The pride of being chosen as class prefect—on merit, on character.

Visiting the sprawling compound of Prof. Yesufu (aka Papa) and hiding behind Dad's solid back as you were pushed forward to greet Papa respectfully.

The best day of the week—nestled between Mum's legs as she unbraided your hair,

massaging your scalp, preparing your crown for the braider in the market.

These whispers of home clashed with England's gaze when you left everything that you knew for an unknown land, where your identity was "the little brown girl from the mud huts in Africa." Do you remember eating pudding before your main meal and not understanding why the kids laughed? You also laughed to mask the sting, beginning a self-protection mechanism that you try to fight against even now. Your crown of braids became a topic of ridicule. Your name, which you held with such pride as it means "Trustworthy," was too hard to pronounce. Your food too smelly. Your skin too dark. Your confidence too conceited.

But Mum wouldn't have it. She saw you shrinking, your light dimming. She continued to braid your hair, using oils to nourish your scalp, and whispered words of love and affirmation to feed your soul. She told ancient stories—wise, magical—singing songs of love and loss that rooted you in who you are. Stories that made you cling to her legs, begging, "Please Mummy, just one more!" as they stoked a fire deep inside.

Dad's role as a doctor brought many new locations and constant change but also built resilience within you. You learnt two truths that serve you still to this day: how to navigate new spaces—and that you would never blend in. Maybe it's the mahogany of your skin or the bounce of your braids you re-learnt how to wear as a crown.

Maybe it's the straightness of your back after Mum taught you: "You are first among equals. Never let anyone tell you otherwise," or your goofy laugh masking when you feel shy. Maybe it's the relentless work ethic inherited from parents who exemplified ambition and grit, or the deep drive to make sure no one ever feels the way you did dear Lilly.

This reminder is for you, Lilly. It's for Mum too—and for my own children, Adanna, Micah, Noah.

To you, Lilly. To Mum. To them.

You will never really fit in. You might want to—and that's okay.

But you don't need to.

I know it. And one day, you will too. I promise.

Amina

Dr. Amina Udechuku
United Kingdom
https://www.linkedin.com//amina-yesufu-udechuku-phd- a1b41722/

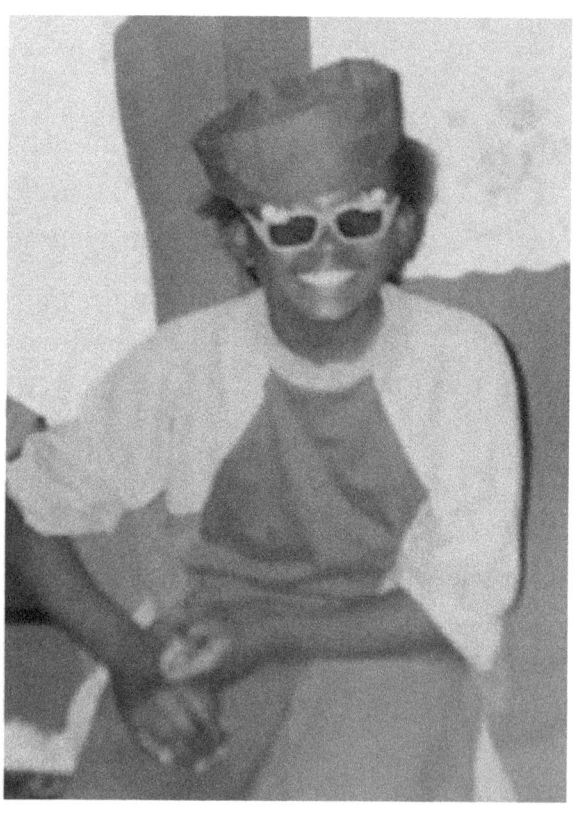

Dear Lilly,

I don't know why I have procrastinated in writing you this letter. I write almost every single day to (and for) friends and strangers without hesitation. The delay is not because I don't have anything to say; in fact, it's the opposite – I have *so many* things to say that I can't decide where to begin.

So instead of one thing, how about a list? A list of things that I would love for you to proactively consider now, rather than reactively learn later. Plus, you'll learn soon enough that we like to choreograph our own rules... Here goes:

1. Perfect does not exist. It simply doesn't. I'm sorry to burst your bubble, and yet I'd really love for you to learn this sooner rather than later. I know that you've spent a LOT of time trying to achieve perfection in a lot of things. That's okay. Let's focus on progress instead.

2. Pick up your head. In your early career, all that focused "heads down" work does allow you to learn so many amazing things. It can also lull you into the dark corner of autopilot and burnout. Schedule in breaks to breathe, dream, and rest. And sparkle.

3. Hold your head high. Yes, I want you to be proud of yourself. It's not vanity; it's acknowledgment. Please be proud of your choices, proud of your strength, proud of your accomplishments, proud of your spirit, and proud of your sparkle. It will all come in handy one day, I promise.

4. Keep trying to fit in. Hang on, hear me out on this one. Contrary to popular belief, "fitting in" really is about fitting in your own skin. It's powerful to know that fitting in your own skin erases the need or desire to fit in anywhere else. Know that your light and sparkle will attract all the right things.

5. Not everyone will appreciate your light and sparkle. And that's okay. Remember when others treat you poorly; it's often more about them than it is about you. It's not your job to convince them otherwise.

6. Lead with and exhibit kindness. Always. Even when kindness is not shown to you, please continue to

show kindness to others and especially to yourself. Please don't allow someone else's actions to dictate how you act and show up.

7. Listen to the voices. Learn to listen to and trust the voice you can hear inside. The voice that wants you to take more risks, to stand in your shoes, to use your voice, to believe in yourself, and to double down on loving yourself. Yep, that's *our* voice, and we are always cheering for you.

Darling girl, you have so many wonderful things ahead of you. I have every confidence in you, and I cannot wait to see what happens next!

Love you,
E

P.S. You know how you can see wonderful things so easily in, about, and for others? Please see those wonderful things for yourself. That's where the magic is.

Eden Ezell
USA
https://www.linkedin.com/in/eden-ezell/

Dear Lilly,

You will wake up tomorrow feeling rejected. You will be teased and made to feel like you do not belong in your school or your neighborhood. Your own brothers and sisters will not seem to respect you the way you want to be respected.

But take heart. A divine plan is being formed for your life; you just cannot see it yet. All you can see is the bullying, the neglect, the confusion. It will not be easy, but you will be able to manage it. If you try to fully understand your current situation, it will not be possible.

But if you keep an open mind and remind yourself that your Plan is still unfolding, then your burden will slowly shift. I know what you're trying to do—you're comparing your life to your friends, your brothers, your sisters, anyone you come in contact with. But that won't make your situation better.

Focus on you. What does Lilly really want to do with her life? What books does Lilly really want to read? Keep asking until you start to see even a glimmer of an answer. I heard you want to be an attorney when you grow up. That's great!

Start asking yourself, "What's the first step I can take to become an attorney?" Wait for guidance from within. Once you know a step, take it. Then ask for the next step. I know you're tempted to ask friends, but they won't be able to help you. The one thing I don't want to see you carry is regret. Mistakes are allowed. Regret is not. Please learn that today.

I know you don't want to disappoint anyone, but I'm more concerned you don't disappoint yourself. Don't chase what others are chasing. They don't even know what they want. Your Plan is already in motion. Let's make sure that Plan is fulfilled. If you get off track, then slowly return to your path. I promise you it gets easier as long as you are consistent.

Wake up every morning to your Plan and watch what happens. And then get ready for an incredible shift in your life.

Your Biggest Fan,
Evan

Evan Benjamin
USA

Dear Lilly,

Years ago, when you wanted to be a psychologist, you took a counseling course to get experience. You aced most of the course except for the first step, which was to reflect what the person said and how they felt. Being someone who thinks fast, you would often see a solution quickly and want them to see it too.

That wife that was being beaten by her husband needed to leave him; yet she couldn't or wouldn't. She was scared and had lost her confidence. The lesson you learned was that to move forward, people need to be allowed to feel and be heard. You also learned that your solution may not be theirs at that point in time, or sometimes ever, and it was far more important to meet people where they are at.

This was role-modeled when your marriage fell apart, and you arrived at work distraught. Your manager asked what you needed and offered to let you be at home, or at work, or even in another country. He gave you the space to feel and navigate a way forward at your own pace. You never forgot that empathy and kindness and the impact it had.

Being forced to reflect on what you have heard requires active listening, one of the most challenging skills there is. This challenge has reared its head many times along your career journey.

When you were asked to mentor young talent, you were eager to share your wisdom and learnings to make their paths easier. You had to remind yourself to listen and respond to what they needed, rather than what you felt they needed to hear.

The most wonderful surprise was how much you learned from those interactions. The young woman who felt "less than" in meetings, surrounded by experienced and qualified men, reminded you to claim your own space in your challenging leadership engagements. The newbies who were struggling to fit into a new workplace reminded you to be friendlier to new employees and learn how to connect with people who were different from you.

What you will learn is that the more powerful and senior leaders get, the more they feel obliged to know all the answers and make decisions on topics even when they are not the expert. As people rise to power, they are challenged less by others and the voices they hear become fewer, allowing them to believe that their view is the only view.

Don't fall into that trap.

Good leaders surround themselves with people better than themselves and tap into those skills when needed. They ask for ideas and feedback and actively listen to suggestions. If you are only hearing the sound of your own voice, remember to go back to that important lesson of active listening.

You are not expected to know everything, and people respond well to being included and consulted. Remember to listen and give space to all the voices in the room, including your own.

Heidi Kornmuller
South Africa
https://www.linkedin.com/in/heidi-
kornmuller-51394915/

Dear Lilly,

You stood frozen just inside the door and would not go in any further. You were scared. You were unsettled. You didn't stray from your spot. You leaned on the nearby shelf to draw with the crayons your teacher gave you.

Kindergarten wasn't what you expected. Your best friend was across the hall in another classroom, and you felt all alone. The teacher checked on you frequently. She would ask if you wanted to join in. You shook your head no, and she left you alone until the next check in.

Although you thought you would never leave your spot, days later, you did. You saw a few other kids playing with a puzzle, and they couldn't find the final piece. You spotted the missing piece and delivered it to them. They asked you to stay for the next puzzle. You joined in and enjoyed it. The next day and every day after, you entered the classroom and sat with your classmates.

For the next several years, you didn't say much in class. Even when you knew the answers, you didn't raise your hand. Your test scores were initially a surprise to your teachers because they didn't know how much you knew.

After college, you volunteered at a non-profit organization. Your hard work led to being asked to chair a committee and eventually being chosen to lead the organization. A new event was being planned and you were excited, until you realized everyone expected you to be the speaker. At that moment, you were the 5-year-old frozen in fear. Then, something strange happened. The physical anxiety felt unexpectedly similar to the exhilarating energy you felt while planning the event. This new feeling needed exploration.

Next, you went to the person whom you heard speak in front of large crowds and seemingly did it without any fears: your dad. He confirmed what you were close to figuring out on your own. Those nerves are a signal of anticipation, not fear. That was an impactful aha moment.

You weren't done yet. Your mom shared the final essential piece. She pointed out how Dad seemed fearless when standing at the podium because he was passionate and knowledgeable about the topic. When you know what you know and you share it with conviction, you deliver a gift to your audience.

Decades later, the nerves remain a constant companion before leading training, speaking in front of a group, or hosting a livestream. Yet they are no longer a red light telling you to stop. Instead, it is the signal that something wonderful is about to happen. The reframed mindset is your power tool.

xo, Leslie Nydick

Leslie Nydick
USA
https://www.linkedin.com/in/leslienydick/

Dear Lilly,

I wish I could tell you this sooner: Love is not earned by exhaustion.

You don't unlock your worth by remaining longer in rooms that diminish you. You don't become more lovable by becoming less yourself.

You learned early that the world can be sharp. You learned to close the door on your own heart. Still, I saw you hold on to hope, looking for signs in dandelions, flocks of birds, and numbers that whisper, "Maybe tomorrow will be different if you try harder, if you're perfect."

My dear, perfection is a mask with no eyeholes. You learned this lesson, and in time, you will completely take it off.

Life and leadership are full of lessons, many of which I wish we didn't have to learn repeatedly. Remember this: When a place stops valuing you, it begins to erase you.

That's the moment to gather your things, not just your cute notebook and keys, but your voice, your rest, your laughter, your intelligence, your no. Especially your no. Pack them away like treasured stones.

And leave.

Leaving is not failure. Leaving is literacy. It means you can read the room and read yourself. It means you trust your body when it tightens at the door, when your shoulders rise like worried shoulders do, when your soul keeps dropping little notes that say, "Not here. Not like this."

I know this feels weighty. You are no longer the child who learned to brace, the teenager who rehearsed apologies for simply taking up space, or the grown woman who turned silver linings into strategy and called it optimism. We are all these versions and so many more unfolding because of a strong ancestral lineage. Our becoming begins with fiercely loving ourselves and knowing that we deserve to be cherished.

Yes, there will be voices. The ones that tell you to stay. The ones that ask you to be grateful for bare minimum crumbs. The ones that mistake your boundaries for attitude. Smile politely. Then keep walking. The floor you're stepping onto belongs to the person you/we are becoming.

Before you go, bless the place for what it taught you: how to spot gaslighting before it flickers, how to find the exit, how to hold your own hand across the street. Memory is not a prison; it can be a map.

And you, my dear, are the cartographer and the wittiest girl I know. On the other side of leaving is not emptiness. It's room. Room for new mentors, better mirrors, work that pays you in joy and not just invoices, friendships that clap from the front row. Room for mornings that don't start with dread. Room for a future you who is so proud you chose her.

You are not alone. We are many, packing our bags with boundaries and walking into our next brave thing. If you can't believe in yourself today, borrow my belief. I have enough for both of us.

With courage that keeps choosing you,
Rohene

Rohene Bouajram
Canada
https://www.linkedin.com/in/rohenebouajram/

Dear Lilly,

Just believe.

Growing up, I had no clear map for my life. I was an accomplished athlete who cared more about sports than school. My parents were divorced, and my mom did everything she could for me and my brother, but I resisted—stubborn and set in my ways. All I could picture was wrestling at the next level; I didn't understand how important grades and planning were. Still, I was determined to be a millionaire before 30, even if I had no plan for how to get there.

You'll work multiple jobs and pick up many skills along the way. Those skills pay off later. Mom and Dad gave you more than material things: Dad, a gifted artist and rock sculptor, taught you the value of connecting with people—"Opportunity comes with how many hands you can shake." Mom, a self-taught, wonderful cook, taught you kindness and the power of listening and learning from everyone. Their quiet wisdom shapes everything you become. Remember their lessons: Build relationships, help others, and always stay humble. Those are the foundations that will support you when plans change.

If I could give you, my younger self, one piece of advice, it is this: Believe in yourself but also prepare. Take responsibility for your education, even if it's not your passion now. Grades and discipline matter because they keep options open. Show up fully to every job, practice, and class—excellence isn't glamorous, but it compounds. Work hard, be curious, and learn from every person and every job you do. Each skill you pick up becomes another tool for the future you haven't imagined yet.

Shake hands, ask questions, and be kind: Relationships open doors you can't foresee. Network not for ego, but to learn and to give. Take more risks; lean into the fear and choose faith instead. When you're uncertain, take small steps rather than waiting for a perfect plan. Failures will happen; treat them as tuition for the next lesson. Resilience, not luck, will move you forward.

You won't become a millionaire in the way you once imagined, at least not yet, but you will become a millionaire in life and faith. That richness matters more than money. Cultivate gratitude, invest in people, and nourish your spiritual life. These are the true measures of wealth that sustain you through the highs and lows.

Keep your determination, but let it be guided by humility, learning, and gratitude. Be open to change, and trust that doing good work and treating people well brings unexpected opportunities. Take steps of faith and trust that God will lead you down the right path—even when you can't see it clearly.

Love yourself, keep growing, and always believe.

—You

W. Temple Haynes
USA
https://www.linkedin.com/in/temple-haynes-87095a92/

Dearest Lilly,

If I could sit beside you right now, I'd tell you to breathe. You don't have to prove anything to earn your place here. You were enough the day you arrived—and you still are.

I know you're trying so hard. You think if you're perfect enough, kind enough, strong enough, maybe someone will finally see you, stay, or love you the way you deserve. You measure your worth by what you do instead of who you are. I get it because I did the same.

But here's what life has taught me: Peace doesn't come from control, applause, or perfection. It comes from learning to rise every time you fall—and realizing that falling was never failure, it was direction.

Courage won't always look bold. Sometimes it's a whisper that says, *"Try again."* Sometimes it's tears on your pillow the night before you start over. Sometimes it's standing in front of the mirror and deciding that today, you'll love the reflection looking back, even if she's still healing.

Failure will show up, more than once. It'll come as heartbreak, disappointment, and detours you didn't ask for. Don't run from it. Sit with it. Let it teach you. Every hard thing will carve you into someone softer, stronger, wiser.

Growth will confuse you. You'll lose people and dreams you once prayed for. But one day you'll understand that letting go wasn't loss; it was clearing space for better things to bloom.

And self-belief isn't something you stumble upon; it's something you build— moment by moment, promise by promise. Every time you keep your word to yourself, you become the woman you were meant to be.

So, when the world tells you to tone it down or take up less space, don't. Be kind, yes. But don't you dare shrink. Speak, even when your voice shakes. Love, even when you've been hurt. Lead, even when no one's clapping yet.

You'll lose titles and roles you thought defined you, but you'll gain something far more precious: *clarity.* You'll learn that being real will always outshine being perfect, and that loving yourself through the mess is the bravest thing you'll ever do.

Keep going, beautiful girl. You don't have to become someone else to be extraordinary. You already are.

With all my love,
Jennifer

Jennifer Perri
USA
https://www.linkedin.com/in/jennperri/

Dear Lilly,

I learned at an early age if I make others happy, don't disrupt, I could avoid conflict, and my life would be less emotionally painful. I trained myself on how to people please and was praised for being such a good daughter, granddaughter, and niece.

On autopilot, this is how I led my life into adulthood, with a smile on my face, doing whatever I needed to get approval. I bent to other people's needs without any consideration of the mental and emotional weight it would place on my shoulders. My self-worth centered around how I made others feel, and I worked so hard to please.

Flash forward a decade and I'm managing a team for the first time. Without thinking, I went back to what was most familiar to me, and I did anything to make my team's lives easier. I was proud when my team spoke highly of me. My flexibility and ongoing support allowed them to grow in their roles because I would step in to pick up the pieces and fill in the gaps. Hearing their praise filled me with joy and self-worth. It wasn't until years later, when I could reflect, that I realized my need to please others not only stunted my psychological growth, but also hindered my ability to grow professionally and as a leader. I focused so much on ensuring my team was fulfilled that I failed to allow myself to learn and grow.

My lesson for Lilly is this: Your personal trauma doesn't stop once you enter the workplace. You can do your best to dissociate from your past, but ultimately, it shapes how you work, collaborate, and lead. It took me a long time to acknowledge the profound impact of childhood trauma on my professional development and career, but once I did and sought the help I needed, I finally had the agency to decide what kind of leader I wanted to become.

Farrah

Farrah T.
USA

Dear Lilly,

You're facing what feels like the worst possible roadblock in your professional career or student life. You've invested countless hours, months of your time, and endless effort to achieve that one goal. Maybe it's a job you really wanted, a university you really wanted to get into, or a career break that's taking longer to turn around than expected. The pain and heartbreak are real, especially when it seems like everyone else has it all figured out.

You wonder why you're not successful, if your life will ever get back on track, and if it's worth chasing your hopes and dreams. On tough days, you might even feel inadequate and think less of yourself.

Let me tell you something important: You will heal. And here's something even more important: You need to allow yourself the time to heal. Surround yourself with loved ones, do things you love—including forgotten hobbies— and be kind to yourself.

You will get back up, brush off the dust, and move forward. Humans are resilient, even if we may not feel like it in our most vulnerable moments. You will see later on that this moment of your life—where nothing seemed to work—was only a small chapter of your life story.

Loving yourself lesson: When life gives you lemons, treat yourself with kindness, compassion, and patience.

Aarshi Tirkey

Aarshi Tirkey
India

Dear Lilly,

For years, I told my story because I thought that was what healing looked like.

I spoke about my childhood abuse.
My complex PTSD.
My years of addiction.

I told it on stages, in boardrooms, and in front of cameras. Each time, I convinced myself it was helping someone else feel less alone.

And maybe it was.
But I didn't realize it was also slowly breaking me open again and again.

Recently, I went on the biggest news station in South Carolina and told my story — the same one I've told for years.
But when I saw it air, something in me cracked.
I started having panic attacks that lasted for days.

Everyone around me was congratulating me for being brave.
They told me how proud they were.
But all I could tell my wife was,
"I feel like I'm bleeding out on a battlefield, and everyone is standing around telling me what a good job I've done."

That was the moment I understood something I wish I'd learned sooner:
People will let you keep sacrificing yourself for them if you let them.

So I made a choice.
I decided I had given enough to this fight.
I had told my story this way enough times.
And I didn't need to keep cutting pieces of my soul out to prove I'd done enough good in the world.

Sometimes, the bravest thing you can do is put down your sword and let the world keep spinning without you for a while.

Because you've done enough.
You *are* enough.
And peace, not pain, is what you deserve now.

With love,
Sims

Sims Tillirson
USA
https://www.linkedin.com/in/simstillirson/

Dear Lilly,

You will face many struggles in life—that is a fact. But please know that these challenges will shape you into the person you are today: strong, kind, and resilient.

Others will try to diminish your self-worth in every phase of your life.

In school, your teacher will throw your artwork across the classroom. You will be made to retake a test after your teacher accuses you of cheating for acing it the first time. You will be humiliated in front of a class of 40 for being last in academic standing. Don't sweat it; you will graduate with a bachelor's degree from an esteemed university and quietly prove everyone wrong.

In your adolescence, you will grow up in a society that values fair skin. You will be ridiculed for your tanned complexion—made the subject of a science lesson, to be laughed at by your classmates, even your best friend. But you will overcome this powerful stigma and stand strong in adulthood.... until your husband (ex now – thank God!) wants a child with another woman. In his drunken stupor, he will call you ugly, dark, short and fat and that you will make a lousy mother. But this too shall pass, and you will meet a man who values your beauty as a person, beyond the superficial.

You will struggle with money. There will be times when you watch your friends enjoy meals you cannot afford. You will return that skirt you love to the rack because your friend says, "Why are you looking at this when you have no money?" You will find yourself wishing for a small lottery win, just enough to pay the bills and eat for the day. You will stand in a Louis Vuitton boutique, breathing in the scent of leather because that is all you can afford. But in time, you will build a life where you can afford what you once only dreamed of.

In job interviews, you may not understand some words used and interviewers will mock your limited vocabulary. Your direct superior will doubt your ability to pass the public accountant certification exams—which you do in just one sitting, secretly hoping that it will be a satisfying slap in her face.

Lesson in Loving Yourself: Others will strive to make you feel less, if you let them. I now know my worth and I deserve everything that I have worked so hard for. I am comfortable in my own skin. I may not know everything, but that is okay. I am financially secure and independent. I love my designer items, but I am the real luxury. These negative experiences have given me greater motivation to be the best version of myself.

Lesson in Leadership: Words are powerful, so think before you speak. There are 101 ways to get a message across—choose the kindest. Share knowledge and lead others so they too can be the best version of themselves at work.

Asfha
Singapore

Dear Little Dreamer,

Letter to a girl who dreamed big in communist Romania

Look at you there.

Eight years old, standing in that queue in the bitter cold, snow up to your knees, your fingers numb even. You've been waiting for two hours now, and you'll wait another hour still, just to buy one orange. One single orange, because that's all they'll allow per person.

But you're clever, aren't you? You'll get back in line three more times, changing your scarf, pulling your hat down lower, trying to look different each time. Four oranges. That's what you'll bring home today. Four small victories that smell like sunshine and taste like defiance.

You don't know it yet, but decades from now, every time you peel an orange, that scent will transport you right back to this moment. To the cold. To the waiting. To the way your mother's face lit up when you walked through the door with all four. To what it means to want something so badly you'll stand in the snow for hours to get it.

That determination? Hold onto it. You're going to need it.

I know what they say to you. "You're so lucky." They'll say it when you get into university. They'll say it again when you finish your degree. And when you land your first teaching job in England, they'll say it even louder, as if luck had anything to do with those late nights studying by candlelight during power cuts, as if luck wrote those papers and passed those exams.

They don't see the work. They see the result and call it luck, because acknowledging your effort would mean confronting their own choices.

But you know the truth, don't you? Even now, as a child, you understand that luck doesn't queue in the snow four times for oranges. Luck doesn't exist under communism, where even dreaming feels like an act of rebellion.

So let them call it luck. You'll know better.

One day, you're going to make a decision that terrifies you. You'll pack everything that matters into one backpack, count out £100—money you earned by working an entire summer—and you'll board a coach to the UK. Not a plane, because you can't afford that. A coach. For three days. Three days of sitting upright, watching the landscape change through a grimy window, every kilometre taking you farther from everything you've ever known. Your back will ache. You'll barely sleep. You'll wonder if you've made a terrible mistake.

You haven't.

You're going to arrive in a foreign country as an au-pair, with your two degrees that suddenly feel worthless because nobody here knows what they represent. They'll see a girl with a backpack and her worn-out copy of Pride and Prejudice and might assume you're running from something.

You're not running from anything. You're running towards everything.

There will be moments when you'll want to quit: when you're cleaning pub toilets, ironing some else's clothes for hours, or cooking for fancy dinners your host family is throwing. When you're homesick and broke and wondering why you left.

But here's what I need you to remember: Every single person who says, "You're so lucky" is telling you more about themselves than about you. They're revealing their own inability to recognise hard work. Their own fear of taking risks. Their own unwillingness to stand in the snow, metaphorically or literally, for what they want.

Your journey isn't about luck. It never was.

It's about a little girl who learned resilience in food queues. Who understood scarcity and fought against it anyway. Who chose to build her future rather than accept what was given.

That girl who queued for oranges? She's still in you. She's the reason you'll succeed. Because you know what it means to work for every single thing you have. You know that the smell of an orange can carry an entire history.

And one day, you'll peel an orange for someone you love, and you'll tell them this story. About the cold. About the small victories. And they'll finally understand that you didn't get where you are by luck.

You got here by being the kind of person who goes back to the queue three more times.

You got here by being brave enough to leave everything behind with £100 and a backpack.

You got here by refusing to let anyone else define your dreams as luck, when you know they're built on sacrifice, determination, and standing in the snow long after everyone else went home.

So here's what I want you to know, little one:

You don't have to smile when they say, "You're so lucky."

You don't have to make them comfortable by agreeing.

You just have to keep being the girl who knows the difference between luck and hard work.

The world will try to diminish you. Don't let it.

Keep dreaming. Keep working. Keep standing in that queue, no matter how cold it gets.

You're going to make it. And it's going to be extraordinary.

I'm so proud of you.

With love across the years,

-The woman you fought so hard to become

P.S. Save one orange for yourself. You earned it.

Cat Marin
Oxford, UK
https://www.linkedin.com/in/catmarin/

Dear Lilly,

I need you to know: "The best is yet to come," and never, ever give up!

I am telling you this because I know the rollercoaster of life can be intense. From the time you were a little girl, not only did you feel that you weren't good enough, but you were also told that by your parents (who were also children having children).

Your parents didn't know how to encourage you. They said awful things to you, and to each other, that no child should have to endure. And when you talked to some of your closest childhood friends about what you wanted to become in life, they told you that you couldn't pursue that career path.

Sadly, you let their words in, and you believed them. You believed you were not enough. Instead of pursuing your dream, you got married and decided to raise a family. This was not a hardship, though, as you always wanted to be a wife and mother. However, you didn't realize that 'happily ever after' doesn't always exist, and one day your marriage would end, resulting in you having to enter the job market with no formal training.

The loss of the marriage and needing to immediately find a job are difficult, especially with your self-confidence being so low… You were trying to build a career, raise a young child, and hopefully find stability. Unfortunately, when you aren't used to having much, you don't expect much… and you don't get much.

You end up spending many years remarried to an abusive alcoholic. You know fear at the deepest levels. You will try to leave and then the promises that he won't hurt you again are made. He breaks those promises and the abuse escalates, until one day when he puts a gun to your head and you beg him to "Do it, just do it."

Thankfully, for you and your daughter, he doesn't pull the trigger. And somewhere during this time, you find your strength; you realize that you deserve more. You ask your landlord to lower your rent while you work through divorce (and he does). You finally find the strength to choose you!

You show your daughter that life isn't always easy, but you are a survivor… and once you begin to believe in your own happiness, to see your own value, you begin to move into the light. Your career begins to progress, your self-esteem improves, and for the first time in a long time, you find your joy again.

Life will not always be easy, but it won't always be hard either. You will experience extreme joy that comes from truly loving yourself. You will forgive people who have wronged you, and you will celebrate many moments of happiness. Most importantly, you will be proud of the beautiful woman (inside and out) that you have always been, and you will understand fully the Bible quote, "Weeping may endure for a night, but joy cometh in the morning."

My Dear Lilly, take comfort knowing that you will know extreme joy and peace! And I am so proud of the woman you have always been!

With love,
Margaret

Margaret
USA

Dear Lilly,

When I got my first job out of graduate school, I called my mom to tell her the good news. She congratulated me and then said about my new boss, with complete sincerity, "Oh, thank goodness it's not a woman."

At the time, I didn't fully understand what she meant. But her relief spoke volumes about the world she had come up in—one where women often competed instead of collaborated. Her generation learned that other women could be their toughest competitors and critics, not their strongest allies.

Thankfully, I've had a different experience. When I decided to leave my full-time role to step out on my own as a consultant, my boss—a woman I admired—referred my first client. Instead of seeing my departure as a loss, she saw it as an opportunity to help me grow. That single act of generosity gave me both confidence and momentum.

Over the years, I've had mentors who have encouraged me, challenged me, and called me into bigger versions of myself. Their words often arrived at just the right time—sometimes as a push, sometimes as a reminder of my worth when I doubted it. And then there are my three best friends from grad school, who remain my inner circle to this day. They are the ones who tell me the truth, celebrate my wins, and remind me who I am when life feels uncertain.

That kind of trusted circle—a group of women who see you fully and want the best for you—is one of the most powerful things you can build. It's not about perfection or constant positivity. It's about honesty, grace, and shared belief in each other's potential.

Supporting other women doesn't mean we always agree. It means we lead with empathy instead of envy, curiosity instead of judgment, and collaboration instead of comparison. It means we celebrate each other's success even when we're still finding our own footing.

The truth is, there's room for all of us to shine. Every time we extend a hand instead of crossing our arms, we chip away at an old and limiting narrative—the one that tells us success is a competition.

So Lilly, and every woman finding her way, don't buy into that scarcity myth. Seek out your circle. Nurture it. And be that woman for someone else. Because when women rise together, the view is so much better.

And maybe going forward, when young women land their first job, their mothers will say about their new boss, with relief and gratitude, "Oh, thank goodness it is a woman."

With encouragement and hope,
Carrie

Dr. Carrie W. Gray
USA
https://www.linkedin.com/in/carriegraydba/

Chère Lilly,

The journey toward la vie en rose is not only possible—it is yours to claim. I write to you as a former femme au foyer who transformed herself into a femme d'affaires—a housewife who dared to imagine a new life and became a businesswoman shaped by courage and reinvention. I am an empty nester now, but long before that title found me, like many other francophiles, the allure of Paris captured my heart. Between raising my children and holding my family together, I found stolen moments to wander through France—the country that first enchanted me when I was 20 years old.

Each return to Paris, Lyon, or Nice felt like a reunion with a forgotten version of myself. The museums, the cafés, the language that curled like music around the ear—all of it awakened something that had been quiet for too long. On every trip, whether during a girls' getaway, family vacation or a solo escape, I caught myself imagining life as an expatriate: mornings with an espresso in the sunlight, afternoons discovering art, evenings writing my own story. But dreams have shadows, and my greatest uncertainty was always this: What about my career? My stability? My family? I wondered how a foreign woman could build a career in a place that stirred her soul. I explored every path imaginable—from becoming an au pair to working as a coiffeuse, even imagining my own beauty salon or art gallery in the small medieval village, Eze. I taught myself French, earned international beauty certifications, and studied with a determination that came from somewhere deeper than ambition.

What I wish someone had told me sooner is this: Sometimes our dreams are simply too big for the people around us, especially the ones who love us. For over 20 years, when I spoke about moving to France, my family brushed it aside. They told me it was impractical, far too risky, and entirely unrealistic. Their fear wrapped itself around my courage until I confused their anxiety for my own. I put my dream on pause, but it never disappeared. Quietly, stubbornly, it followed me. Every French class, every certificate, every degree I earned was both preparation and proof—to them, and perhaps to myself—that I was capable.

And then, two months ago, I did the thing no one expected. I traveled to France, scheduled meetings with realtors to view housing options, and placed an offer on a condo in the south of France. The offer was accepted. Just like that, the dream I once whispered became something I could hold in my hands. If there is anything I have learned, Lilly, it is this: Never place your dreams on hold to make others comfortable. Fear can be inherited, but courage can be chosen. It took me 20 years to untangle myself from a fear that was never mine. You do not have to wait as long. Your dream is not too big. It is simply waiting for you to grow into it.

Bisous,
Alicia

Alicia Hilaire
Louisiana, USA
https://www.linkedin.com/in/alicia-hilaire-phd-candidate-27485a11b/

Dear Lilly,

You are happy-go-lucky,
full of dreams,
full of opinions about right and wrong.

You wear the good girl tag proudly,
believing kindness is enough to live in this world.

You don't know what lies ahead,
but you believe it will be good.

You believe doing the right things
will guarantee a smooth life.

Why would it be any other way?

Then, life happened.
It looked nothing like you expected.

You let others' opinions shape your choices.
You played by the rules because that's what they expected.

And somewhere along the way,
their voices grew louder than your own.

Here's what I want to tell you today:
You are never just a good girl.

You are smart, strong, and resilient.
You have dreams, very big ones.

And you know how to go after them.
Don't let anyone's definition of "good" shrink your spirit.

Don't confuse being kind with staying silent.
And don't ever let go of that hope,
the one that makes your eyes sparkle when you dream.

Don't let anyone dim your light.

You might fall, and that's okay.

But know that you will find your way.

Each time a little wiser,
a little freer,
and a lot stronger.

So here's to you:
to chase your dream,

to walk through the storm,
and to become exactly who you were meant to be.

Here's to the girl who never stopped believing!

With love,
The woman you became.

Regards,
Sajina

Sajina John
India
https://www.linkedin.com/in/sajinajohn/

Dear Lilly:

The struggle never truly disappears. It shapeshifts. It matures with us, evolves with every scar, every lesson, every year we keep walking.

You learned this early. Growing up in a poor and violent household in Mexico, then crossing illegally into the U.S. and returning again, hopelessness was not a stranger; it was almost a roommate. Yet even at nine years old, you refused to surrender. You didn't know the word *resilience* then, but you were already practicing it. That stubborn spark, that tenacity, would become one of the most valuable assets in your entire life portfolio.

When options were few and kindnesses even fewer, you carved out a refuge where none existed: school. Academics weren't just the "way out"; they were survival, identity, oxygen. And fortunately, even fatefully, your mind was wired to thrive there. Knowledge became your passport for everything you aimed for.

The road was anything but smooth: doubt, fear, oceans of insecurity. Encouragement was rare; gentleness scarce, it even had to be self-taught. But you pressed on. One scholarship after another. Excellence not as vanity, but as necessity.

Then came your Master's scholarship abroad. It wasn't luck. It was the logical outcome of a lifetime of preparation disguised as struggle. Cross the ocean with a gifted one-way plane ticket, and suddenly, the fight changes shape again. It's no longer about surviving; it's about becoming. About allowing a dream to take up space in your chest. About stepping into a better version of yourself you hadn't yet dared to imagine.

And yet, the past leaves traces. Out of ignorance, fear, sadness, and sheer need, you made choices that now sit heavy with shame. Shame that still whispers, still slows you down, still convinces you you're an impostor in your own story. Like many others, you've often been your harshest critic, convinced that one day, someone will uncover the "hypocrite" you believe yourself to be.

But here's the quiet truth:
The struggle didn't break you—it shaped you. Your story isn't about perfection. It's about the evolution of struggle—and of the person who learned to turn it into strength.

Lesson in Leadership:

Your journey—raw, messy, illuminating—has granted you something many people never develop: amazing powers of observation and empathy. These didn't appear overnight; they were forged through every hardship, every emotion, every moment you had to read the room to survive. Over time, this became a superpower: the ability to listen not just with your ears but with your whole presence. Use these gifts. Let them guide you in understanding the people you work with, in seeing the nuances behind their struggles, in supporting them toward their fullest potential. Leadership isn't about walking ahead; it's about walking with.

Lesson in Loving Yourself:

If the struggle evolves, then so must you. You can't become a better version of yourself while clinging to an outdated draft. Your past mistakes, as uncomfortable as they may be to revisit, were not detours; they were curriculum. They shaped the very person now striving for growth. So show yourself some empathy. Embrace the earlier you, not because everything they did was right, but because everything they did brought you here. And no, embracing your past doesn't mean repeating it; it simply means honoring the distance between who you were and who you've become.

Mit freundlichen Grüßen / Best regards
Maria

Maria Solis
Mexico
https://www.linkedin.com/in/maria-solis-nogueda-8582409a/

Dear Lilly,

You know... sometimes life doesn't fall apart because you did something wrong.

Sometimes it falls apart because your heart is trying to make room for what's right.

For a long time, I thought I was doing everything the *right* way. I married my high school sweetheart, built a life, chased "happily ever after" the way I thought I was supposed to. And when it didn't feel right—when the sadness crept in, when my body screamed what my heart couldn't say—I thought the answer was simple:

A fresh start.
A new town.
A new house.
A new chapter.

We moved again and again, believing peace lived in the next destination. I packed my hope into cardboard boxes and carried it with me, hoping the next place would finally feel like home.

But here's the truth nobody likes to say out loud:

You can't outrun a life that doesn't fit you.
No matter how many times you start over, the same story follows you… until you finally listen.

My body knew long before my mind did. The nausea, the dizziness, the exhaustion, the aching sadness—I thought I was sick. I even convinced a doctor I was sick. But I wasn't. I was breaking in silence.

And then one day… I realized the bravest thing I could do wasn't staying and trying harder.
It was leaving, even when it terrified me.
It was choosing myself so I could be the mother my little boy deserved.

And the strangest thing happened—the moment I walked toward truth… the symptoms disappeared. My body exhaled, and so did I.

And then life surprised me in the most beautiful way.

I found something I never believed I'd truly have:

A love that feels peaceful, not painful.

A home filled with laughter, honesty, kindness, and the kind of warmth you don't have to earn—you just get to feel.

A partner who doesn't just love me—he chose my son too, with joy and devotion, like his heart had been waiting for us all along.

We found each other again—my best friend from college, a familiar laugh, a safe place I didn't recognize the first time around. And now? Now he's my husband. He's my son's dad. He's the chapter I didn't know I was waiting to read.

We joke that our life is a Hallmark movie—except we earned every soft moment, every laugh, every happily-ever-after day by day, choice by choice, breath by breath.

And if there's one thing I've learned, it's this:

Sometimes your body whispers the truth before your heart is ready to hear it.
Sometimes love looks like leaving first so you can learn how to receive something better later.

And sometimes—the fairytale begins the moment you stop running… and finally come home to yourself.

Shaley

Shaley Buss
USA
https://www.linkedin.com/in/shaley-buss-590537298/

Dear Lilly,

When did we stop dreaming?

I suspect it happened around the fourth or fifth grade. The moment we were told to start being *realistic*. Dreams shrank into checklists: Get into a good college, get married, buy a house. Those aren't dreams; those are instructions.

I was the kid who always took the road less traveled: curious, bold, uncontainable. And then life happened. Bills to pay. Expectations to meet. Reality hit like a ton of bricks, and my inner warrior took over. She got things done. She protected me. She built the life that kept the lights on.

But here's the truth I didn't see coming: The warrior can only build; she can't breathe. For more than two decades, I forgot what it felt like to want something *just because*. To go somewhere not for work, not for someone else, but for the adventure of it.

Five years ago, at 42, I took a trip for no one but me. It started as an act of quiet defiance post-divorce. A trip my ex-husband once refused to take. I went anyway. What began as rebellion turned into awakening.

Planes, trains, buses, cabs, water taxis—every new form of motion unlocked an old part of me. The girl who once daydreamed in class was back at the window, watching the world go by and wondering, *What else is possible?*

Dreams started to seep out through the cracks; timid at first, then louder. They weren't gone; they were waiting for permission.

My lesson for Lilly is this:
The warrior may build the walls that keep you safe,
but the dreamer is the one who will set you free.

So let her back in.
Let her whisper what's next.
Let her remind you that not every journey needs a map.

Unrepeatably yours,
Susan

Susan Throop
USA
https://www.linkedin.com/in/susanthroop/

Dear Lilly,

For more than 30 years, I lived under the quiet weight of fear: fear of failure, fear of rejection, and fear that I wasn't enough. I spent decades feeding those stories instead of feeding my faith. I told myself I was too introverted, too unqualified, or too late to become who God created me to be.

Then, in 2023, everything in my life came to a halt.

In April, I celebrated a major victory: I paid off our home nearly 18 years early. But just one month later, my sister was tragically killed in a head-on car accident. In June, my marriage was tested, our business revenue became unpredictable, and I realized I had placed more trust in my work than in God.

Those months broke me open. They stripped away comfort and control and forced me to reflect on my direction, my values, and who I was truly trusting. In prayer and silence, I could finally hear what God and

Jesus had been whispering to me for over 30 years: *"You've spent your life helping others grow, now lead them with your voice and your faith."*

When I stopped striving and started surrendering, everything changed. I began to see that the years I thought were wasted weren't wasted at all, they were preparation. Training for leadership, humility, and obedience. I finally understood that my calling was to help others lead with integrity, faith, and courage to show people that fear and faith cannot occupy the same space.

Now, in my fifties, I'm an executive leadership coach and keynote speaker. I've spoken at conferences across the U.S., been a guest on numerous podcasts, and built friendships that stretch across the world, including Australia. I pray with clients, speak to leaders about purpose, and encourage executives to align their work with God's truth.

Life still has challenges, but it feels lighter because I no longer walk alone. I walk with peace, purpose, and confidence that I'm doing what God designed me to do.

If you ever find yourself questioning your direction, remember this: **You are not late, you are being prepared.** Sometimes God clears out what's comfortable so you can finally hear Him clearly.

Don't waste decades doubting yourself like I did. Trust that what feels uncertain might be the very moment God is aligning your life with His calling.

Faith doesn't remove the storms, it teaches you how to fly through them.

With purpose and peace,

Cory

Cory Dunham
USA
https://www.linkedin.com/in/corydunham-executive-leadership-coach/

Dear Jordan,

You have twinnies on the way...
Here's what you need to know to keep sane.

You are enough.
You are doing enough.
You are enough exactly as you are.
But God loves you far too much to let you stay that way.
It's time to buckle up. Life is going to get tougher.
Put on a helmet and get ready to get tackled. Hard.

Ask for help sooner than you want to.
Sleep whenever you have the time.
Forget about the things that don't matter.
Sleep, walk, read, pray, repeat.

Go above and beyond only when you're able.
Say no when you need to.
Say yes when they need you.
Say, "It's okay" when you choose wrong.
Say, "Gimme a sec" and then pull yourself together.

Put your head down and take one action.
Tiny stones will bring down even the biggest castles.
Keep throwing pebbles one day at a time.

When you fail, write it down.
When you succeed, write it down.
When you aren't sure, write it down.
Bring words to life to never forget.

Call Mom.
Talk to a friend.
Cuddle with your beautiful wife.
Not later. Now.

And when things get really hard:
Play a game.

Take an ice bath
Bake a pumpkin loaf.
Don't forget what works.
Never backburner your mental health.

Because there is no finish line for becoming.
There is only improving.
And you have all the time in the world.

So get ready to soar onward and upward.
To gallop into the great beyond of parenthood.

To experience life more vividly, more presently, and yes, more painfully.

With stubborn hope and more than a little gumption,

-Jordan

P.S. Give today your best yes because that's all we can ever do.

Jordan Ring
Lisbon, Portugal
https://www.linkedin.com/in/authorjmring/

Dear Lilly,

I grew up in a Nigerian village where the deepest poverty was not of money, but an acute barrier to information. The path was pre-written: "School is a scam. Learn a trade." Surrounded by this chorus, I believed it. I apprenticed as a tailor, treating school as a side hobby—a place to pass the time, not to build a future. My ambition was being neatly tailored by the limits of my environment.

Then, a seismic shock, literally. We were accustomed to those "Lagos-Boys-News" claiming dubious super-genius performance, but a boy from my own village—a boy I played football with in the very same dust—achieved the impossible: straight As on the WAEC, our gateway exams. My mind raced for an explanation. He must be faking! He must have a secret tutor, a wealthy uncle, *something*. The alternative—that such brilliance could emerge unaided from our reality then—was too disruptive to accept. Driven by a desperate hope, I knocked on his door that SAME evening. "How did you *really* do it?» I pleaded, searching for the hidden trick. He simply shrugged. «You know me, I just read what I could find here."

The simplicity was revolutionary. His parents were a trader and a farmer. There was no secret, no performance. No "faking it." He hadn't talked about success; he had quietly built it, page by page, through sheer determination, courage, and resilience in one of the most remote places on the planet. Remember, there was no internet. In that moment, he wasn't just a student; he was my first true leader. His action was his authority.

His example became my permission slip. If he could, then I must and I *can*. I traded doubt for well-read textbooks. I trekked miles to lay my hands on hard-to-find Further Maths and Chemistry books—from which I got myself a permanent nickname till today. Two years later, I didn't just pass; I broke the city's record. The ripple was instantaneous. The village's mantra shifted from "It's impossible" to "If he can do it, so can we." I had sparked a revolution without a single speech.

This "lead-by-doing" ethos became my compass, my leadership hallmark. At university, my actions spoke louder than any campaign promise, leading to multiple elected positions. When colleagues dismissed the grueling CFA exams, my journey through them in record time became a roadmap, inspiring a wave of new charterholders. My path to Yale wasn't a performance; it was a demonstration of the cumulative power of authentic, intentional action.

The lesson is clear: People have a flawless radar for pretense. They are inspired not by titles or perfect speeches, but by the raw, honest evidence of someone striving and succeeding. Leadership is not about having all the answers or being perfect. It's about embodying the pursuit at hand honestly and authentically. When you stop performing and start *doing*, you don't just command respect—you grant others the courage to follow their own path.

Stop faking it. Start building it. Lead by doing.

Kolawole S. Adegoke
Nigeria
https://www.linkedin.com/in/koladegoke/

Dear Lilly,

I want to share the most important lesson I've learned about ambition: A dream isn't something you *have*; it's something you *do*.

We often assume we have to wait for the perfect degree, the big job, or the official title before we can start living out our dreams. I made this mistake too.

I spent years letting life direct me, getting stuck waiting for my degrees to open the right doors to becoming a psychologist. Even after I was accepted to a PsyD program and offered a prestigious summer internship at Yale, my gut told me to say no to both. I felt completely lost, but that feeling led me to a crucial realization: When I gave up the *idea* of the dream, I found the *action* that was meant for me.

That action—career counseling—was a perfect fit for my true gifts and talents. My dream didn't disappear; it simply morphed into something better.

The key to this transformation is the difference between finding and creating opportunities.

I learned this from an art student who approached me out of the blue. He wasn't waiting for a gallery to call; he simply asked if he could donate a piece to hang in my front office to feature it in public. He created a public showcase for his work out of thin air. Finding the right opportunities often only comes *after* you've started creating your own.

If I had created small opportunities to "do" psychology earlier, I would have realized much sooner that my best path wasn't in clinical practice but in helping others find their careers.

The most common trap I see people fall into is getting stuck on a future thought: the dance student who wants to teach but never volunteers to lead an after-school class, the engineering student who never organizes a small public showcase of something they've built, the photographer who never creates a special town history exhibit for the town hall.

Don't look to do your dream in the future. Do your dream *now*, in whatever small way your life allows.

Start teaching, start building, start showcasing—even if it's just in a corner of your current life. By living your gifts today, you will have success long before you reach your final destination, and you will allow your initial dream to grow into one that is even better than you ever imagined.

I know mine did.

Onward!

Joanne Conrad
USA

To My Dear Lilly,

As you grow older, I hope you always take time to notice the small moments: the smell of coffee in the morning, a walk on the beach, your favorite song on the radio, the warmth of a hug. That's where joy hides, in the little things.

Don't rush through life chasing what's next. Celebrate the little wins along the way. Life isn't waiting for you in some big milestone; it's happening in the journey, in the here and now.

Don't dwell on the past either. There will be times when things don't go as planned, when you'll wish you could go back and do it differently. When that happens, don't stay there. Take the lesson, carry the wisdom, and move on. The past is meant to teach you, not to define you.

And when challenges show up—and they will—try to see them as invitations to grow. It's not easy, I know. But even the hardest moments carry a gift, a push to become more of who you're meant to be. Gratitude, even in hard times, will carry you through.

Wake up every day with intention. Every hour, every moment is a new beginning. A chance to start again, to choose differently, to see life through a lens of trust and gratitude. Most importantly, give yourself grace through it all. You don't have to have it all figured out. Keep learning, stay open, lean on others for help and support, and always show up! Growth lives in discomfort. Feel the fear and do it anyway; that's how courage is built, one step at a time.

And above all, always remember this: YOU hold the power to choose the kind of life you want to live. No matter what life throws your way, you decide how to see it, how to react to it, and what meaning to give it. That choice will shape everything.

So, my dear Lilly, may you choose to create a good life, not a perfect one, but a meaningful and intentional one. One filled with love, presence, peace, laughter, and grace.

Remember, "Life is 10% what happens to you and 90% how you react to it." – Charles R. Swindol

With love,
Rola

Rola Hassanieh
USA
https://www.linkedin.com/in/rolahassanieh/

Dear Lilly,

It's been quite a journey! When I started, I remember having spunk and confidence. I've been told I was unafraid to enter a room, and I always found a friend. I signed up for everything and was confident I had what it took to succeed every time, even when my parents said the odds weren't in my favor.

But then… what happened? It all changed, and suddenly, I didn't want to enter the room, I couldn't find a friend, and I didn't want to participate. I remember who defeated my confidence. I remember the times that hurt, the times that I was left out or ignored, and so I didn't want to try anymore.

Lilly, let me just say, while I can blame the world, I also know I let myself stop believing. I let others define me and what I was capable of doing. That, my dear friend, is a long and lonely road. But good news, you don't have to go down it!

I'm still working on believing in myself every day again, but mostly, now I'm good. I have talents, and I'm good at the jobs I have and the titles I hold. Some people might not like the words I write, but that, as a good friend of mine used to say, is why there's chocolate and vanilla; not everybody likes everything.

So let your spark shine! Some will be supportive, and others just won't get it. Does that matter to you? No! Because you like what you do, you like who you are, and you know you have what it takes to succeed in your life.

And one more thing, Lilly, remember to be that support for others. When you feel like you're not quite measuring up, sometimes it's easy to feel like tearing others down will make you feel better. But that will not work; it never has. Help others to thrive, and you will find that, magically… somehow, you will too.

With love and throwing all my support your way,
Heather

Heather Martin
United States
https://www.linkedin.com/in/heather-martin-711518117/

Dear Lilly,

I have been trying to find belongingness since the womb, and since my mother can attest to all her children as unwanted births, I have a blood attachment to being *lost, disconnected, and unseen.* Let me explain.

Trauma psychology and epigenetics tell us that a baby's first experiences in utero are touch—they're feeling the pressure, the touch, the pulsation of heartbeat of the mother, the breadth of the diaphragm. Touch is five times more specific, more potent, more primary than words because when we touch each other, we are reading what a person is experiencing. This leads me to realize that the environmental pressures that existed when I was in utero were a lot louder, more potent, and more emotionally transferable because of how often my mother was unsafely touched by an unpredictable father. Additionally, before my mother, many of our foremothers had all been seduced, abused, and abandoned too. I was born deprived and frustrated. My mother can tell you I came into the world sad, furrowed, and listless.

Children stuck in the dorsal vagal mode at birth are seen as showing a shutdown state: are numb, dissociated, hopeless, helpless, feel abandoned and unwanted. I say again, I have been looking for belonging since the womb.

My genetic origins, sourced from various forms of abuse, recover more slowly from trauma, avoid connection, and are less prone to socially engage. And, unfortunately, because my surroundings as an infant were shaped by fear, it was safer to socially disconnect and develop an existential sense of humiliation and shame. While the self-esteem of adults who have attained internalized sources of pride can survive the withdrawal of love from others up to a point, it appears to be difficult, if not impossible, for a child to gain the capacity for self-love without first having been loved by at least one parent or parent-substitute. And when the self is not loved, by itself or by another, it can die. In Fall 2014, I tried to.

Up to that point, I had spent much of my life an alien to myself. Not only was I alien to the physical space we occupied in the U.S. as immigrants, I was also alienated to the darkest corners across racial, economic, language, and gendered lines. Above the repressed feelings from colonization, historical trauma, and family abuse lay undiagnosed symptoms of depression, anxiety, substance use, and PTSD.

Dearest Lilly, by attending to our early life from birth to early adulthood, we learn a lot about our basic predisposition toward leadership. Today, after years of meditation, contemplation, and catharsis, I write to you from a place more ethereal than where I was. My present day understanding of my past is to overcome, or radically accept, the amount of displacement in my life and not let severe self-doubt overshadow my love and sense of wonder.

Nowadays, I try to lead in a way that leaves lasting substance.

Stay in touch,
Isis

Isis J. Lara Fernandez
USA
http://www.linkedin.com/in/isis-j-lara-fernandez-ms-phd-candidate-a4225a3a

Dear Lilly/Sue,

Everything you've been experiencing, from teasing to family challenges to the relentless drive to prove yourself, is building emotional intelligence, resilience, and leadership that will serve you well.

You were only four when you accidentally overheard your mother confiding to her friend, *"I'm so sorry I couldn't give Bob the son he always wanted."*

While confused and saddened, you became determined to show your dad that girls could do anything boys could do.

Then, at age 10, came the terrifying night of your mother's first mental breakdown. From then on, you had to grow up too fast to help care for your two younger sisters whenever your parents couldn't. At school, you became a perfectionist, trying to control what you could.

For years, you thought your emotional sensitivity was a weakness because you cried too easily and felt everything so deeply. Eventually, you'll discover that it's your superpower. Your ability to sense others' needs and connect with empathy will help you become a more successful, purpose-driven leader, innovator, and investor.

Many times, you've been underrated. You were small and teased as a "shrimp." Plus, your asthma made playing sports extra challenging. Yet, through years of effort, running laps before or after practice to make up for your slow pace and lack of endurance, you eventually became a cheerleader, gymnast, lacrosse player, and soccer player.

Your father had limiting beliefs that only boys were serious athletes, so he failed to recognize your efforts. However, you were always worthy, even if you didn't feel it. You only need to prove yourself to yourself, not to those who underestimate you.

Remember your Grandfather Bevan who told you, *"Girls can be anything they want to be."* He recognized your math and science interests, then encouraged you to become an engineer because, *"Engineers learn to solve tough problems and make our world a better place."*

People may judge you through clouded lenses due to their own limited views. Please ignore voices trying to make you feel small or powerless and walk away from anyone who overlooks or undervalues your talents.

Instead, seek out those who share your aspirations to advance more life-improving innovations, empower more people to live with purpose, and create a more inclusive world that's better for all.

Any pain you experienced has not been wasted. Every challenge has taught lessons that transform lives—yours and many others. Your experiences prepared you to thrive in male-dominated fields, to lead with both strength and compassion, to help others break through their own limiting beliefs.

One day, you'll realize that these experiences gave you powerful drive. That navigating your mother's mental illness gave you resilience and emotional depth. That your "nerdy" curiosity and "shrimp" size never limited what you achieved.
Keep believing in yourself, even when others don't.

You're not too much or too little. You are exactly who you need to be.

Our world needs your gifts. You'll spend your life empowering others to access their own.

With love,
Your Future Self

Sue Bevan Baggott
USA
https://www.linkedin.com/in/suebevanbaggott1/

Dear Lilly,

In 2020, I thought I had everything I ever wanted. The world was changing, jobs were coming and going, and chaos seemed to be everywhere. Yet somehow, I was living my dream: a new relationship, my first corporate HR position, and working from home for the first time.

To many, "living the dream" means owning a home, being married, and starting a family by your thirties. But my dream didn't look like that—and I'm proud to say, I'm okay with that.

You see, I grew up in a small rural town in the Midwest. To shop at Target, we had to drive an hour and a half. To order pizza, 25 minutes. Life was simple… but it was isolated. I didn't have a strong support system. I had dreams—posters of my dream college hung on my wall—but no one cheering me on.

When I said I wanted to go to college, I was told I couldn't handle it because I was in special education. I remember that heartbreak like it was yesterday. But then, a teacher saw something in me. She walked me right back into that counselor's office and said, *"She can and she will."*

That moment changed everything. Someone believed in me—and that spark lit a fire I've carried ever since.

From that day on, I learned to advocate for myself. I took college courses, I worked long hours as a CNA, I went to church alone, I served as a summer camp counselor for 10 years—and slowly, I built a life of my own.

Then came the night that changed my life forever—Christmas Eve, 2006. I was supposed to sing a solo, and my mom was supposed to come. She didn't. I broke down moments before going on stage. But a kind pastor, dressed in a white robe, wrapped her arms around me and said, *"Everything is going to be okay."*

And somehow, I found the strength to sing.

That night, God placed new people in my life—people who loved me, took me in, gave me a place at their table, a stocking on their mantel, and eventually, helped me get to college. They became the family I never had.

Fast forward—I graduated from the college of my dreams in 2013. Life has brought its share of storms since then—losing my mother to suicide, leaving a toxic relationship, getting laid off—but every challenge became a chapter in my story.

And now, as I sit here—single, no kids yet, in a hotel room with my golden retriever by my side, praying for the next job, the next home, the next step—I am filled with gratitude. Because this is not the end. It's a new beginning.

I'm starting my graduate degree in Human Resources Management. I'm rebuilding my life with peace, self-love, and faith.

And I share my story today because someone needs to hear this:

You are not defined by your circumstances.
You are not your past, your pain, or your setbacks.
You are your persistence, your purpose, your faith.

So, write your own story.
Sing your own song.
Because you belong.

You've got this, girl. I'm rooting for you.

Many blessings,
JoDee

JoDee Lantz
USA
https://www.linkedin.com/in/jodeelantz/

Dear Lilly,

When I was diagnosed with a Grade III brain tumor, I thought the hardest part would be the treatment—the radiation and chemotherapy. The truth is, the hardest part was learning how to face the new me each morning. I had to meet the lady that God was shaping me to be— one stripped of many things familiar to me, including my hair, not once but twice.

The first time I went bald, I tried to be strong for everyone else. I smiled and said, *It's just hair* and tried wearing wigs. The second time, I was more prepared and I met God in a deeper way than I ever had before... in my entire life.

It was in quiet mornings that I began to encourage myself *through Christ.* I learned to speak His Word over myself. I began declaring Philippians 4:13 (AMP): *"I can do all things [which He has called me to do] through Him who strengthens and empowers me."* As well I reminded myself of Jeremiah 29:11 (AMP): *"For I know the plans and thoughts that I have for you," says the LORD, "plans for peace and well-being and not for disaster, to give you a future and a hope."*

I also clung to Psalm 46:1—*"God is our refuge and strength, a very present help in trouble."* His presence became my peace, His promises my hope, and His power my source of courage.

Lilly, I want you to know that it's okay to feel weak sometimes. Strength doesn't always look like smiling through the storm. It's holding onto Jesus when everything else feels uncertain. The world may not always cheer for you, but Heaven is standing with you. And in those moments when no one else is there to lift you up, Christ will whisper to your heart.

Learning to encourage myself through Christ changed everything! It taught me that my worth isn't tied to my appearance or achievements—it's anchored in who I am in Him. The same power that raised Jesus from the dead lives in us (Romans 8:11), and that means no diagnosis, no loss, no hardship can take away the purpose He placed within you.

If I could tell you one thing, Lilly, it would be this: Draw near to God in every season—especially the hard ones. Talk to Him like you would your closest friend. Tell Him your fears, your frustrations, and your dreams. He will meet you there with love that restores and peace that surpasses understanding.

So, when life feels heavy or your reflection looks unfamiliar, lift your head and remind yourself: "I am still here, and God is still good." You are not alone. You are deeply loved. And through Christ, you can encourage yourself again and again—until your strength begins to shine from the inside out.

With love and faith,
Rachel

Rachel McCants
USA
https://www.linkedin.com/in/rachel-mccants-motivational-speaker-b457b582/

Dear Lilly,

This is a difficult situation, and it takes immense courage to face it. My guiding principle when encountering unacceptable behavior or inappropriate comments at work is simple: Speak up.

I'm truly sorry you had to experience this. I can only imagine how challenging it must be to be in an environment that feels unwelcome and disrespectful. It's natural to consider leaving—sometimes the weight of it all feels unbearable, and protecting your peace becomes the priority. If that's what you choose, it's completely understandable.

Above all, put yourself first and do what feels right for you.

That said, I encourage you to consider speaking up. I know—it's hard. It's frightening. You may worry things could get worse, fear backlash or retaliation, or wonder:

What if I share my experience and no one believes me? These concerns are valid.

As a well-loved quote says, "Help will always be given to those who ask for it." While support isn't guaranteed, there are times when help arrives swiftly and abundantly. There are people—inside and outside your workplace—who will make you feel heard and seen. They will do everything to support you and stand by your side.

If change doesn't come, I'm deeply sorry things unfolded this way. But remember: what you did was brave. By speaking up, you showed that silence is not an option—because silence only empowers those who harm others.

Loving yourself lesson: Your voice matters.

Aarshi Tirkey
India

Dear Lilly,

Showing others who you really are takes courage, vulnerability, and a lot of faith. Courage to be open, vulnerable in allowing people to know you on a far more personal level, and faith that you will not be judged or treated differently after the fact.

Where do I even begin writing to my younger self? Am I addressing the seemingly happy-go-lucky fourth grader who rides her unicycle or the young girl who witnesses things because of her parents' addictions that no child should see and go through? Am I addressing the teenage girl who loses a parent to suicide, gets married, and has a baby all during high school? Is this letter to the young professional who so often was told she will never succeed or grow in her career because she does not have a degree, and was passed over for promotions and new jobs solely because of the lack of paper rather than her proven merit and work accomplishments? Is this to the career professional that at some point struggled with learning something new but later found it was more about how the information was being taught? I am writing to all of you.

There is so much I wish you could have known when you experienced these things. There will be many hardships and tribulations, as with anything in life, and at times you will feel incredibly overwhelmed. But there will also be many accomplishments and experiences that bring you joy and success.

On a personal level, you will walk across that high school stage having not only graduated as a junior but done so with a new baby. You will not become the "statistic" of a child of addicted parents or that of a teenage mother who did not finish college. (It really is OK and it's never too late if you change your mind, by the way). You are not the things you endured in your past. You will learn to accept help from friends and family when you need it the most. You will lose many loved ones, and friendships may come and go, but next to your children/grandchildren/family, you will develop relationships that stand the test of time and are immeasurably treasured. Never take your loved ones for granted as your time with them is limited.

On a professional level, you will learn to adapt in the workplace, and your ability to work in multiple roles within an organization will allow you to grow professionally in ways you could never imagine. You will come across many bad colleagues in the workplace and deal with sexual harassment and generally poor behavior. However, you will also be blessed with some of the best colleagues and bosses who encourage you, mentor you, and become your dearest friends. You will endure a very lengthy layoff and come out far stronger on the other side. Difficult roles have developed you into a strong performer and leader in your own right. Stop doubting yourself. You are smarter and far more capable than you give yourself credit for.

How I wish so many things had been different for you. But those challenges made you who you are today. You were never as alone as you often felt, and you are not alone today.

Leadership Lesson:
You may never truly know the real story behind the professional persona of your employees and colleagues. Remember the Golden Rule and treat others as you would want to be treated. While recognizing not every hire is perfect (which we have all seen on more than one occasion if we are honest), be mindful that it will often lead to success for both the company and the employee when you take time to discover how best they learn. Play to their strengths while equally, and without too harsh criticism, supporting their growth in areas of weakness.

Loving Yourself Lesson:
When you look back on your life, you will be incredibly proud of how far you have come. Things always work out as God had intended for you. Keep the faith. Your success rate for getting through every bad day in your life so far is 100%. Take the time to cherish each accomplishment for what it is.

My dear Lilly, I leave you with this quote you will live by for over 15 years strong, and still going: "When feeling overwhelmed by a faraway goal, repeat the following: I have it within me right now, to get me to where I want to be later." –Karen Salmansohn. And never forget, "You have to accept whatever comes, and the only important thing is that you meet it with the best you have to give." –Eleanor Roosevelt. To thine own self be true.

With love,
Heather

Heather Demshock
USA
https://www.linkedin.com/in/heatherdemshock/

Dear Lilly,

I am so sorry to share that you developed an undiagnosed syndrome which will cause you many problems throughout your career.

The good news is that in your late thirties, you finally uncover what has been impacting you for years... and oh how I wish it was understood earlier.

My dear Lilly, you suffer from imposter syndrome. You spend your early career worried that you aren't good enough, believing that your luck will run out, and fearful that someone will recognize that you really aren't as talented as you have been given credit for.

The demons from the past (including shame, the fear of being stupid, and fear in general) continually attempt to derail you.

Let me assure you that you are talented, and let me further confirm that you are not a fraud. More than anything, let me confirm that you are not alone. This syndrome cripples all too many professionals at some point in their careers. I've read that as many as 70% of the workforce deal with imposter syndrome. Who knew?!

Worse, instead of talking about and identifying this syndrome, it too often remains a secret. This causes many, like you, to rely on the "fake it `til you make it" mantra. Women who you have always admired will finally begin talking about this, and you will be shocked to learn that Maya Angelou, Meryl Streep, Michelle Obama, Kate Winslet… all suffered from this same syndrome at some point in their careers.

Please hear me: You are not a fraud. The professionals that hire you know what they are doing!

The cure for this syndrome isn't found in a prescription; rather you must continue to believe in yourself every single day. You WILL shake this (most days), but it will take longer than it should as it is truly a lifelong battle.

Leadership Lessons: With imposter syndrome impacting 70% of the workforce at some point, shouldn't we begin educating students now? And if we aren't teaching this within our curriculum, let's begin talking about it in offices, in company newsletters, in professional organizations. Imagine what ideas and creativity might be unleashed in an organization when people aren't worried that their ideas may not be good enough or that they aren't good enough.

Lesson in Loving Yourself: This is a hard lesson to articulate so I am going to share what someone once said to you: "Ali, I really wish you could see yourself the way that others see you." Those words helped you get a career coach to really examine "Am I enough?" Spoiler alert: You are! Believe!

With Love Always,
Ali

Dear Lilly,

Age is a great equalizer. When you're young, you think you know how to do everything and don't think there's anything left to learn. Then, you have a misstep, and you're paralyzed with how to deal with it. You don't want to let others know for fear of seeming weak. You think you know how you'll handle things.

That just makes it worse. You may be smiling on the outside, but you're sad on the inside.

Then, one day, you start to write down your raw feelings. Before you know it, the raw emotions bubble up. Each day, you add to your personal journal. In time you come to grips with your situation and you move on.

As you get older, you realize that one misstep becomes multiple missteps through no fault of your own. You come to realize that's what life is. Nothing stays constant. You realize you can't control as much as you think. You're also able to better put things in perspective.

Welcome to life.

I was fired from my first job and thought it was the end of the world. It was, but not for the reasons I thought about when it happened. At the time, I didn't think anyone would ever hire me again. I was a failure. In time I realized that while I was a failure, it was because I was doing something I hated doing.

You learn more from failure than you ever will from success. You learn about yourself, about your passions, and what you really want to do.

To this day, I go back to my first journal (handwritten) and re-read it. Many of those words are just as relevant now as they were then.

Those things I used to stress out about are meaningless.

Life's too short.
Ken

Kenneth Lang
USA
https://www.linkedin.com/in/langk/

Dear Lilly,

Leadership has taught me to embrace it all, even the messy middle.

Here's your permission to exhale, to feel it all, and to welcome even the parts that don't go according to plan.

There will be seasons when things go sideways. When that new leadership role shakes your confidence. When change moves faster than your footing. When you're juggling so much that slowing down feels like dropping the ball. When your cape falls off.

But here's what I've learned: Those moments aren't failures; they're invitations. The messy middle isn't a setback; it's the space where growth takes root. It's where you begin to see what really matters, what needs to be released, and who you're becoming in the process. So take a breath. Let it unfold. You don't need to have it all figured out right now. The path will reveal itself. That's the magic of the messy middle.

And please, don't try to do it alone. Build your circle—the people who remind you of your strength when you forget. Let them show up for you, just as you do for them. That kind of support isn't weakness; it's wisdom.

My lesson for Lilly is this: Embrace the mess when it hits, and it will if you are leading a big life! Growth happens through the mess! And, for heaven's sake, let others help you, just as you will help them!

Love,
Amy

Amy P. Wilkins
USA
https://www.linkedin.com/in/amypwilkins/

Dear Lilly,

I turned 58 this month, and when I look back, I see a lifetime spent chasing something I never needed in the first place: approval.

For so many years, I believed that if I could earn the acceptance of others, especially those who were indifferent or unkind, then I would finally feel worthy. I thought their validation would make me whole.

But here is the truth I want you to know early: Seeking acceptance from people who do not care for you is a trap. It steals your voice, your joy, and your sense of direction. And in trying to become "enough" for them, I lost myself, personally, professionally, and spiritually. The heartache wasn't in their rejection; it was in the parts of myself I abandoned along the way.

There will always be people who do not like you, who do not understand you, who are threatened by you, or who choose not to see you. And that is a fact. No amount of shrinking, performing, pleasing, or bending will change their minds. All it will do is exhaust you.

What I know now that I wish I had known then is this:

- You were already enough.
- Your worth is not a vote.
- Approval is not love.
- And acceptance that requires you to disappear is not belonging.

Wisdom, I've learned, often arrives dressed as mistake, regret, and hindsight. And yes, you will make your own share of mistakes. You will say things you wish you could unsay, stay in places you should have left sooner, and give your heart to people who never earned it. That is part of being human. Do not let shame silence you.

When you realize you have gone down the wrong path, turn back with courage, not embarrassment. Reach out to the people who matter, especially those who have consistently shown up with compassion and truth. Apologize when you must. Forgive when you can. And most importantly, forgive yourself.

If I could place one lesson in your hands, it is this: Protect the parts of you that make you: your voice, your curiosity, your softness, your stubborn hope. Hold onto them fiercely. Do not trade them for applause.

With love, hard-earned clarity, and the confidence I wish for you,

With best regards,
Sanjukta Shams (Shama)

Shama Shams
USA
https://www.linkedin.com/in/sshams-cfre/

Dear Lilly,

Here's what I wish I knew when I was your age. Your body is your greatest leadership ally. It holds wisdom that your mind may be slow to process. Cherish it as your most precious possession, because it is. Without your health and well-being, you suffer and so does everyone around you.

Knowing this, I want to share with you three lessons I learned later in life that can save your most important relationships and thousands of hours of productivity.

First, your brain registers body sensation before thought and emotion. Seriously. Research shows 80-90% of your vagal nerve fibers send messages from your body to your brain, telling you whether you are safe and secure or scared and anxious.

Second, your physical body position cues your brain for safety or fear. Try this. Think of something you want to create in the world. Hunch over while making two fists. Think of your project and notice what thoughts and emotions arise. Now raise your eyes to the horizon. Reach out the top of your head, open your chest and shoulders, think of your project, and notice what shifts. You likely noticed concern first and then opened to possibilities.

The third truth is the game changer: Repetitive movement builds your muscle memory for how you respond under pressure. When you were young, you likely learned to tighten your body and prepare to fight, run, or freeze in place. This is normal. But now you have a new choice. Rather than respond from fear, you can reset in an instant and respond with confidence, clarity, and resilience.

Here's how I retrained my body to lead with composure and clarity. Use these four simple shifts you can make in five seconds. If you do this two to three times in your day, your body will learn to make this shift even when everything feels crazy. I call these the GROW practices to reclaim your calm in an instant:

Ground. Place your feet flat below you. As you press into each foot, feel your spine get taller.

Release. Let your arms relax by your side. Take extra-long exhales (which lower your heart rate) and envision any tension rolling down to the ground.

Open. Broaden the space in your chest, roll your shoulders back. Slowly turn your head to the left, through the center, and to the right to open your perspective.

Wander. Shift your eyes from your screen to the space. Imagine you are looking at a beautiful sunrise. Let your eyes rest on the horizon.

This is the way to GROW your capacity to be thoughtful, caring, and connected with yourself and others, even when everything feels like it's falling apart. When you show up as a calm and composed person, you help calm all the nervous systems around you. Even in a crisis, you're all ready to solve the problem together with your best thinking and creative open hearts.

With love and hard-won wisdom,
Kimberly

Kimberly S. Arnold
USA
www.linkedin.com/in/kimberlysarnold/

Dear Lilly,

Do relax your grip on life.

Often through the pursuit of achievement, we strive for perfection. A look, a career, an outcome. Upon not (read never) achieving perfection, our minds can spiral into rather dark places, as if we are not good enough for our own perceived perfection. Furthermore, we take this out on the people closest to us and on ourselves. Perfection simply doesn't exist. Yet we hold this so tightly.

The older you get, the more you realize that tight grip of life not only is exhausting, but it is also born from fear. Fear that you might be seen as incompetent, fear of losing relationships, fear of not being seen, fear of letting someone down, that may or may not even be with us today.

And in an incredibly counterintuitive way, loosening this grip will allow more of the right stuff into your life and on your path. Because others notice. They might not consciously point to why, but when you are walking your path comfortable, balanced, and assured, others are drawn to this. Opportunities seem to pop up more often as your field of vision has widened, and people see your high degree of self-respect.

Should the very notion of easing your grip send a chill down your spine where your physiology is pushing back, this could be a call to work on you first, instead of proving to the world you can [fill in the blank]. A great framing might help too. The world wasn't made for you. You were made for the world. So go be your best self.

Just like auditioning for a play, it can be nerve-wracking. But the casting director wants to see what you can do, not what you're afraid of.

Relax your grip and watch your true path unveil itself.

Your evergreen supporter,
Mark Holden

Mark Holden
USA
https://www.Linkedin.com/in/markholdencfp/

Dear Lilly,

If you don't raise your hand, people might not notice you.

You spent too long trying to blend in. In college, you'll learn the value of raising your hand to share your opinion in class. This will translate to the workplace. You'll see how sharing your ideas can help improve processes and contribute to the success of the business.

You know that being a dominating voice is not what makes you seen and successful.

You'll learn to listen before you speak. Most importantly, you'll learn what's happening in the business, what's important to leadership, and what your colleagues are working on.

You'll let all of that information roll around in your brain and develop into meaningful ideas that you share and drive forward.

One day, your team's leader will leave the company. The department head won't have a plan. You'll come in the next day with a Post-it note of ideas for how to move forward. You'll raise your hand and say you can do this job. Because you can.

All of your previous practice raising your hand will give you the confidence for that most important hand-raise of them all. That hand-raise will give you the chance to show what you can do and propel you to the executive leadership level.

From there, you'll grow even more and start mentoring others. Helping others grow will be the most rewarding thing you've done so far!

You'll face challenges along the way. You'll be told again and again by some people that you can't do it. You'll do it anyway.

And then you'll go on to do even bigger things. I promise, it all happens! You'll be amazed at the reputation you build through years of hard work and contributing in a valuable way. Shockingly (to you), people will reach out to you about working with you, or refer their friends and colleagues to you. All because you raise your hand and say you're here to help.

Lesson in Leadership: Even quiet people have ideas. Find a way to help all types of people participate. Encourage them to find their voice and to speak up so they can grow and achieve their goals. Coach them or help them find the right coach.

Lesson in Loving Yourself: Consider feedback but don't let it define you. Think about where that person is coming from, whether they're qualified to make that assessment, and if there's something you can take away from it. But don't let negativity define who you are and hold you back. You have the power to grow in the direction that's best for you. You can do it!

Laura

Laura MacGregor
USA
https://www.linkedin.com/in/lauramacgregor/

Dear Lilly,

You won't believe how fast the world will change.

Not in decades, but in blinks. In clicks.

One day, you'll look up from your screen and realize you've crossed a bridge you didn't even know you were building: from intuition to innovation, from being guided to being the guide.

You'll work alongside machines that can mimic intelligence, but not empathy.

And you'll learn that your humanness, your grace, your discernment, your ability to feel deeply and decide wisely are the very thing technology can't replicate. Don't hide that. Lead with it.

You'll be told to move fast, to optimize, to scale.

But remember that not everything sacred can be accelerated.

Slow down enough to feel what's true. Lead like a lighthouse: steady, grounded, casting light even when the sea looks wild.

You'll discover that leadership isn't loud; it's listening.

It's showing up with integrity when the algorithm rewards shortcuts.

It's reminding people, and sometimes even AI, that success without soul is just noise.

And Lilly, please don't apologize for being soft.

Soft is not weak.

Soft is how steel remembers its purpose to protect, not pierce.

Soft is how you build trust, heal teams, nurture ideas that last.

The world will try to measure your worth in titles, metrics, or market share.

But your true legacy will live in the people who felt seen because of you: in the small businesses you lifted, the women you mentored, the ethical lines you refused to blur.

One day, someone will ask what it felt like to be a woman leading through the birth of artificial intelligence.

And you'll smile because you'll know the real story was never about AI learning to think.

It was about humans remembering how to *feel*.

With love,
You—older, wiser, still curious.

Naomi Caietti
USA
https://www.linkedin.com/in/naomicaietti/

Dear Lilly,

I know right now it feels like the world is pointing out everything about you that makes you different—your lips, your thighs, your body—and turning those gifts into something to laugh at. I know it hurts when they call you "watermelon lips," not realizing, or maybe not caring, how heavy and cruel those words are. I know those moments make you question your beauty, your belonging, even your worth. But hear me when I tell you this: There is nothing wrong with you. You are not too much of anything, and you are certainly not less than anyone. You were made exactly as you were meant to be—every curve, every feature, every ounce of you is intentional.

One day, you'll see what Mama meant when she said people would pay big money for the lips you have, and you'll smile—not because they finally caught on, but because you'll have learned what she already knew: Your beauty was never theirs to define. The world will shift its standards again and again, but you will remain unshaken because your confidence will grow from something deeper than trends. It will come from knowing that you are rooted in something unchangeable—your history, your family, your soul.

Little one, remember this: No one stands above you, and no one stands beneath you. You walk beside others as an equal, grounded in your worth, and steady in your grace. So when the teasing comes, when you feel small, hold your head high. The very things they mock today will be the same things that make you magnetic tomorrow.

And more than that, they will remind you, again and again, that you were made perfect, inside and out.

With all the love and pride in the world,
Darreisha

Darreisha M. Harper
USA
https://www.linkedin.com/in/dmichellespeaks/

Dear Lilly,

I may only be midway through my career, but I know one or two things about being a young female finding her way around the corporate world.

I started my career as an in-house legal and compliance officer at a subsidiary of the Central Bank of Malaysia. I was tasked with the impossible responsibility of building a legal and compliance department from scratch. My alarm bells went off when I heard that they couldn't retain someone for the job for more than six months due to the sheer volume of work and pressure the role entails, but God bless my naive heart because I followed Richard Branson's famous quote: "If somebody offers you an amazing opportunity but you are not sure you can do it, say yes—then learn how to do it later," and said yes to everything. It was a baptism by fire, and I inherited a desk that felt far too big for someone who still looked like she might be the intern.

Very quickly, I learned two things: No one hands you credibility and, especially as a young woman, you have to walk into the room carrying your own. At 24, I thought that meant changing up my tone to make it seem like I'm older than I was, hiding away my pink and cutesy notebook and putting up a stern composure—it worked like a charm! I began winning many favorable terms even though my counterparts were financial institutions and had higher bargaining power. I now know that it was not the illusion of age or my subdued femininity that helped me score my contracts; it was the conviction in what I was saying that lent me the credence. Wisdom is not reserved for those at the end of the road—never let experience, image or anything for that matter take away what you can truly offer to the world. Everyone brings something unique to the table; find what you do best and show up confidently.

Years passed, and I found myself in a senior position for a tech start-up. This job landed me a seat at the 'big boys' table: management meetings, where I would be the only female amongst several other men who were at least a decade older than me. But being a young Head of Legal and Compliance, I often had to hold my ground on subjects that may not have been party favorites, and there were many a time my views were brutally shot down. I took it on the chin but never allowed my voice to quiver. What I learned is to always maintain integrity in everything you do and speak. Though it may not help you win Miss Personality, it sure does drive value to the people around you and the job that you serve. If nothing else, it helps you sleep better at night.

Along the way, there will be those who question your capability, citing your youth, or speculating whether motherhood will be in your five-year plan in a subtle attempt to make you feel small, but I'm here to tell you that you will learn to silence the chatter and focus on what matters. Just never forget to give yourself grace through it all.

I am still learning and steadying my voice, but these days, I move forward with all of me, no matter how inadequate I sometimes still feel.

Lavannya
Malaysia
https://www.linkedin.com/in/lavannya-manickam-842563132/

Dear Lilly,

What if I told you that there is only one person on this planet who you will be with from cradle to grave. From birth to transition. And that person is YOU!

Wouldn't it then make a whole lot of sense to dig as deep as you possibly can into what makes you... you!

Self-love can only come through self-awareness. You can't love someone whom you don't know.

The most important relationship you will ever have in your lifetime is the relationship with yourself.

There is no greater form of self-care than self-love.

Here's how the math breaks down:

There are just over 8 BILLION humans on planet Earth, and there is only one of you!

So, in the immortal words of Dr. Seuss: "Be who you are and say what you feel, because those who mind don't matter, and those who matter don't mind."

Falling in love with yourself first doesn't make you vain or selfish, but does make you close to indestructible!

Stay flawsome and thrive,
Doug

Doug Skoke
USA
https://www.linkedin.com/in/dougskoke/

Dear Lilly,

You will be told, again and again, that networking is important, and that it is a crucial skill to build your career. You are young, smart, and eager. So, every now and then, you reach out to someone to set up a coffee, or you ask for an informational interview.

You are nervous. You've been doing this job for six months (a year if you count the internship). They've been doing this job for 25 years!

Despite your nerves, the coffee goes great! Look at you networking! At the end, they ask for your resume.

The next day, you are busy, and you forget to send it. A week goes by. Maybe two. You start to think that too much time passed. After all, you don't want to seem pushy or rude. They were kind enough to meet you for the coffee, and you don't want to bother them. You are so early in your career; you tell yourself you are not really worth their time. You trick yourself into forgetting that they *asked* you for it! They *offered* their help.

You never send the resume.

Then, somehow, one day you are on the other side of the table. You are wrapping up a coffee with someone young, smart, and eager. You hear the words come out of your own mouth: "Please do send that article on carbon capture once it comes out."

You want to impart upon her how important this is, that this moment could lead to another, and another. That three months from now, your old colleague might mention that they need someone tracking carbon capture technology regulations.

You want her to understand how unfortunate it is that so often, there is never really any follow-up. The resume doesn't get sent. The article doesn't get shared. You want her to understand that it's okay if it is a week later. You want to tell her that sometimes you wonder how many opportunities you missed when you were young, because you didn't want to bother people—people who were perfectly happy and willing to help you.

You want to tell her that the people who are sticky, the ones who send the follow ups, who check-in two months later to update you on their new role—those are the ones that you remember. And those are the ones you end up helping.

Leadership Lesson: Don't be shy, and follow up. You can bother people, especially if they invite you to bother them. You are your best advocate, whether you are job hunting or just trying to find out where a file was saved. You are going to have to bother people a lot in your career, so start now!

Loving Yourself Lesson: When people offer you their time and attention, accept that you are worthy of it. I am rarely bothered when people reach out to me, and I hope that you realize you were never a bother at all.

Always,
Kate

Kate Rustici
USA
https://www.linkedin.com/in/kate-rustici/

Dear Lilly,

In today's complex business environment, leadership is not defined solely by vision, decision-making, or operational excellence. While these are essential, one of the most impactful qualities a leader can possess is *empathy*. Empathy is not a soft skill; it is a strategic capability that drives engagement, retention, and performance across the organization. It is the ability to understand and share the feelings of others.

Empathy in leadership goes beyond just showing up to meetings. It is being present for our teams: truly listening, understanding perspectives, and acknowledging challenges. This creates trust and psychological safety, and these are the foundations of high-performing cultures. When leaders demonstrate empathy, they unlock discretionary effort, foster innovation, and strengthen resilience during times of change. It means actively engaging, asking questions, and showing genuine interest in the challenges and successes of those around you. When team members know their leader cares, they feel empowered to contribute their best work.

Developing this skill requires intentionality:

- Listen to understand, not to respond.
- Create space for dialogue and transparency.
- Model accessibility and authenticity.

Empathy is not about reducing accountability; it is about enabling people to perform at their best because they feel valued, respected, and supported. As leaders, our presence and attentiveness signal that we care, not only about results but also about the people who deliver them. It doesn't make leadership easier; it makes it more meaningful. It transforms workplaces into communities where people thrive.

As leaders, you set the tone for the culture. Take time to connect with your teams in a meaningful way—whether through a one-on-one conversation, a check-in during a meeting, or simply asking, "How can I support you today?" Your presence and empathy will ripple through the organization, creating a stronger, more resilient team.

Let's commit to lead with empathy every day, because leadership is not just about guiding; it's about connecting. It is not just good leadership; it is good business.

"Leadership is not about being in charge. It is about taking care of those in your charge." – Simon Sinek

Warm regards,
Christopher

Christopher Snow
USA
https://www.linkedin.com/in/christopher-snow-377959a/

Dear Yancik,

Hi. I remember you—the girl who watched more than she spoke, who felt deeply but kept it neatly inside. You will spend years trying to make sense of that quiet. Eventually, it will become your compass. It will guide you toward a life that's yours alone.

The world will often move faster, louder, or more chaotically than feels right to you. You will crave solitude when others thrive on noise, you will prefer reflection to reaction, and independence will feel like home even when it's misunderstood. In this discomfort, you will find your curiosity, your perceptiveness, and your grounding. You will notice details many miss—the subtleties of space, the nuances of conversation. This will form a mosaic of ideas, perspectives, and quiet conviction, giving you texture and making you intriguing in ways loudness never could. The steady way you listen, your quick wit, and the depth behind your words —when you do choose to use them—will draw people in. You will become perfectly yourself.

Your quiet strength echoes the lessons of those who came before you: people who learned to survive by listening more than speaking. A child of Jewish refugees from the USSR, you proudly carry generations of endurance within you, and with it, an unspoken pressure to honor a family that crossed oceans, adopted unfamiliar cultures, and lost parts of themselves so you could have choices they never did. You will soon decide that gratitude must look like achievement. That sense of responsibility is a gift that will give you strength to reach the kind of success that may feel unimaginable right now—career, stability, recognition... even hard-won pride.

Through it all, you will often be misunderstood. Those close to you will equate togetherness with presence— meals, visits, long conversations. They will mistake your need for space as distance, your independence as disconnection. But solitude is the panacea you will forever need to effectively return to the world with clarity and motivation. One day, you will appreciate that love does not have to look loud or constant to be real. You will see that your rhythm—time in, time away—is not a flaw to fix but a truth to honor.

As life winds on, your quiet will be where you process the contradictions of life's unexpected turns, of two cultures and two identities. You will honor your roots without being bound by them. You will love your family without becoming their reflection. You will belong to your heritage and still build a life that is your own.

But there will be nights when the room feels too quiet, even for you; when the joy in your heart will still feel out of reach. This is not failure. Some dreams will remain untouched, some paths will never open—but none of that will diminish you. You will be a success, not in spite of the life you live, but because of it. You are never out of step; you simply move to your own rhythm, one the world is only just beginning to hear. You are the product of courage, resilience, and love that crossed borders and generations to reach you—and you will honor all of it best by being wholly, unapologetically yourself.

Yana
New York, USA

Dear Lilly,

Leadership has taught me that storms are unavoidable—but chaos doesn't have to be.

For too long, I believed the only way to prove my worth was to keep grinding, keep fixing, keep carrying everyone else's load. The truth? That wasn't leadership. That was survival.

What shifted everything was learning to pause. To breathe. To choose curiosity over control. To trade the illusion of perfection for the reality of authenticity. I stopped hustling to belong and started daring to become.

My lesson for Lilly is this: Leadership isn't about being the loudest voice in the storm. The calm in the storm isn't about being untouched by it—it's about refusing to add to it. That takes guts. That takes empathy. That takes loving yourself enough to stop shrinking or pretending.

When we lead from that place, we remind people (and ourselves) of something essential: We were never meant to do this alone.

Unrepeatably yours,
Susan

Susan Throop
USA
https://www.linkedin.com/in/susanthroop/

Dear Silence,

I'm Using My Voice Now

For a long time, I believed that staying quiet kept me safe. I learned early that silence could protect me from many things: from conflict, from judgment, from pain. But over time, that silence began to protect something else too: my fear of being seen.

When you grow up in chaos, you become an expert at reading the room, anticipating reactions, and keeping the peace. You learn to survive by shrinking yourself. Even after you grow up and leave that environment, those instincts follow you. It can lead to intrusive thoughts, whispering that your voice doesn't belong in the room, that you have to prove yourself before you speak, that your confidence is something you need to earn.

That's what impostor syndrome feels like. It's the echo of old wounds, convincing you that you're an outsider in spaces you've already earned the right to stand in.

I know now that leadership requires your voice. It requires the courage to speak the truth, to ask hard questions, to challenge systems that depend on our silence. For years, I mistook people pleasing for professionalism and overworking for worthiness. I thought my quiet meant humility, but really, it was fear.

Healing taught me that walking away from chaos is leadership. I began to understand that the same instincts that helped me survive my childhood could also help me lead. Instincts such as the ability to listen deeply, to sense tension before it surfaces, to hold space for others. But what I was missing was the ability to pair those gifts with the one thing that I had been denied, and I had long denied myself: my voice. Coming to that realization and being able to start practicing that changed my life.

Every time I spoke up, even when my voice shook, I reclaimed a piece of power I didn't know I still had to take back. I stopped apologizing for existing in rooms I had already earned the right to enter. I began saying what I actually felt, rather than what I thought everyone wanted to hear.

Dear Silence, you once kept me safe. For that, I thank you. But safety is not the same as peace. Peace is found in truth, in speaking, in standing, in using my voice to make space for others who are still finding theirs.

To anyone who has ever doubted the value of their voice, know that your story matters. Your perspective is needed. Your leadership begins the moment you decide that your words carry weight.

I am no longer afraid of the sound of my own courage. I am using my voice now, not to fill the room, but to remind others and most importantly, my daughters, that they belong in it too.

Erica

Erica M. Cochran
USA
https://www.linkedin.com/in/ericacochran/

Dear Lilly,

When I was young, I felt invincible. Getting an illness that could threaten my life never crossed my mind. Like most ambitious professionals, I was focused on climbing the corporate ladder, believing that accolades would prove my worth. I was chasing success, not realizing what I was sacrificing along the way.

At 26, I was accepted to Wharton, the #1 business school in the country, newly committed to a woman I'd been friends with for seven years, and navigating the excitement of living in NYC. Then life knocked me off that ladder with two shocking words: testicular cancer.

The idea of not being able to have children terrified me more than dying. I was sure the woman I had finally committed to would leave. I remember the night, sitting at the kitchen table after surgery, breaking down as I said, "If you're going to leave because I might not be able to have kids, do it tonight."

She looked at me and said, "We'll adopt. I want to build a long life with you. Having you live is what matters most." That moment changed everything. I realized she loved me for who I was, not what I did or could do.

Seventeen years later, that dreaded cancer word would come back to taunt me, but this time, it was my wife's turn. Sharon was 43. We had two kids then, ages 9 and 12, conceived the old-fashioned way (after all).

Now the tables were turned. Sharon was diagnosed with advanced breast cancer, and in an instant, I saw life through a different lens. For years, we had faced everything as a team, raising our kids, building our family, and dreaming of the life we designed for retirement.

I didn't pray for success; I prayed for time, enough time for her to see our kids graduate high school.

We got that gift. Sharon's now 15 years into survivorship, and I'm 32 years into mine. Our scars tell different stories, but they share the same truth: gratitude for every day we get to watch our kids grow up.

Looking back, those two cancers were the best gifts I ever received because they gave me the one thing success never could: perspective.

Before my wife's diagnosis, I used to think, "High school is when I'll take the time to build relationships with my kids." Thank God those cancers forced me not to wait, because what began as fear became the lesson that changed my life.

Lilly, no job title, money, or recognition will ever outshine the relationships you build, especially with your spouse and children. Those bonds are formed when you're young, not when you're established and successful.

Don't wait until you've "made it" to nurture what matters most. Life doesn't wait. Sometimes, you don't get the second chance I did.

If you're lucky to reach old age, know this: Your real legacy isn't what you achieve. It's who you love and how deeply you love them.

With gratitude for every scar,
Rich

Rich Keller
USA
https://www.linkedin.com/in/richskeller/

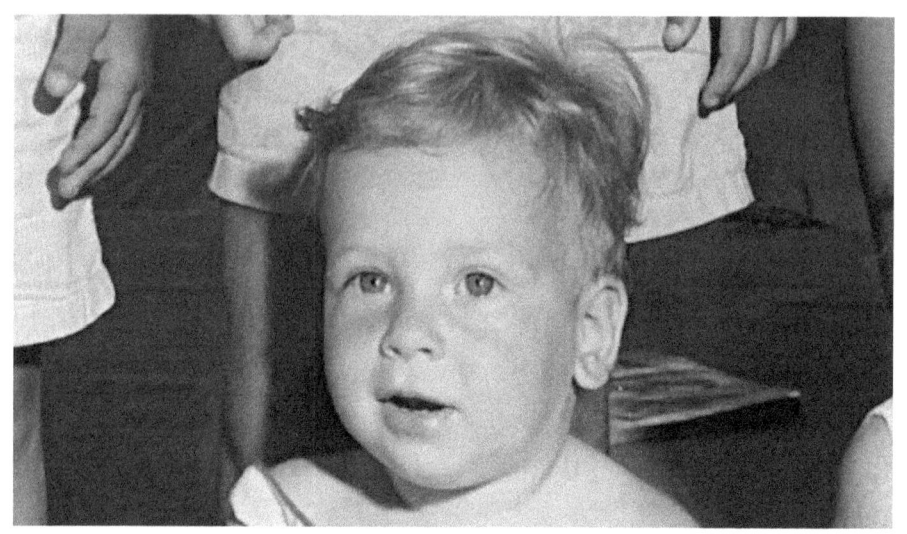

Dear Lilly,

You will have moments that change you.
The day you lose your father, and the world tilts in a way that never quite returns to center.

The day someone tells you to be careful what you say.

The day you realize that no amount of achievement can quiet the inner voice that keeps asking, "Am I enough?"

Those moments will break you open. And for a while, you'll do what you've always done, you'll work harder, push through, try to stay strong. But eventually, you'll learn that strength isn't holding it all together. It's being honest enough to admit when you can't.

In those moments, keep growing.

Growth is staying awake when it is easier to move through on autopilot. It's the awareness that comfort can become a cage, and that sometimes, the hardest questions are the ones that break something open inside you. Allow yourself to change your mind and evolve without apology. Every version of you has done the best she could with what she knew. Growth is honoring her—and still not staying her.

Growth is about grace, not grind. You will get stuck in the belief that if you work harder, someone will notice. But grace will show you that effort isn't the only way forward. Grace creates space for being human, for not having it all figured out, and for trying again without shame or judgment. It allows you to keep growing without needing to prove that you are.

Growth is leadership in motion. It's not about the position you hold but about how deeply you choose to listen with curiosity, to challenge with courage, and to learn with humility. Leadership isn't a level to reach; it's a responsibility to deepen. When you lead this way, you expand others, not just yourself.

Growth keeps you alive to possibility. Your story isn't over, and reinvention is always available. The next chapter is yours to write, and it is not defined by who you were, but by who you are still becoming. There is freedom in knowing you can change direction without losing yourself.

That is why I want you to keep growing. It's not about doing more; it's choosing to see and choose differently. It's what happens when you stop protecting the parts of you that got hurt and start using them to see more clearly, lead more deeply, and believe more freely.

You do not need to be fearless. You just need to be willing. To love, to lead, to try again, to begin again.

And when you look back years from now, you will see it all differently—every detour, every heartbreak, every quiet, hard-won moment of courage — it was not just the road to where you are. It was the becoming.

Keep growing because life is calling you to be more of who you already are.

You'll become someone you'd be proud to follow. And she'll still be growing too.

With love,
Amy

Amy J. Clark
USA
https://www.linkedin.com/in/amyclarkgmlg/

Dear Lilly,

High school alienated me, and surely life would start making sense in my twenties. In my late teens, I worked part-time for the Federal government while attending college, and leadership was a nebulous thought. My wise 40-something GS-12 supervisor once asked me what I wanted to do in life, and I honestly had no answer.

She clearly was in control of her life with all the answers. Nobody had ever asked me that question before, professionally at least. As the lowest employee on the totem pole and newly minted neophyte, everyone else stood 15 feet tall with all the answers. Age and experience surely would bring answers. Please, twenties, where art thou?

Come my twenties, I graduated college, switched government jobs, and meandered. Not knowing what to do in life, I continued with my job as an AIT instructor, a role with authority but devoid of leadership. My military supervisors stood tall as USMC Captains and Majors in their late thirties, crisp uniforms and heroic tales, valor: HOORAH—all the ingredients for great leadership. Oh my… Where did I fit in with all of this? My thirties would bring answers.

Come my thirties, I joined the commercial side. Military supervisors replaced by civilian leaders in their forties and fifties, big job titles, corner offices with windows, arrogance, misplaced courage—traits I mistook for wisdom and leadership, which I assumed carried along with it the noble intentions that so often accompany it— so I thought. In hindsight, I came across great leaders, military, and civilian, but far and few in between. My forties surely would bring answers; they had to.

Come my forties: wash, rinse, repeat. Different co-workers and leaders, same job titles, personalities, pontifications, and arrogance; *Do as I say, not as I do*, not a stiff upper lip in sight. Wait a minute, I see a pattern here. For the past 20 years, I worked with a few great and inspirational leaders, but what about the remaining 75% who…weren't? Was I wrong all these years about leadership? What is leadership after all? Are there gray areas? Am I on to something? I must be; I am in my forties. But wait, how can I be a good leader if I don't know what that word means?

Something clicked as I approached my fifties. I had a moment of clarity along with a transcendental experience, driven not by a single event but the sum of them all. My fifties later confirmed it. I am almost there.

Leadership is not an attribute; it is a noun, until you come across a true leader. But what makes a true "leader"? To quote Supreme Court Justice Potter Stewart regarding pornography (a quote I will take artistic liberty in extending to define "leadership"), "I know it when I see it."

There can be a fine line between arrogance, incompetence, courage (feel free to add additional nouns to the list), and leadership. Hindsight really is 20/20! I came to the realization that, throughout my career and evolving optics, my interpretation of leadership was often as clouded and confused as I was. I saw numerous corporate and military leaders make grave mistakes, often driven by arrogance, incompetence, being unqualified… to name a few. Maybe some just did not have that leadership DNA in them. "Fake it 'til you make it" served so many so well.

I believe we make leadership decisions (sometimes split-second with profound implications) throughout our lives based on information we have at that moment in time, mixed in with optimism, fear, anger, arrogance, bias, humility, unknowns….

Leadership is not all about addressing problems, leading and inspiring people, being compassionate, or making the right decisions. It is not necessarily attributed to age, wisdom, or experience. It is about humility, commitment, saying (sometimes internally), "I don't know," holding yourself accountable, and being true to yourself. I am not a better leader today than I was in my late teens. It is OK not to know, and it does not matter if someone is a better (although subjective) leader than you.

Maybe now I have answers, or maybe I do not—no more than when I was in my twenties. Maybe that's leadership! Paraphrasing what philosopher Bertrand Russel once said: "The problem with the world is that fools and fanatics are always so certain of themselves, and wiser people so full of doubts."

What type of leader are YOU? I believe it is not all about what you project and how it *affects* others, but rather about your true inner self and how you harness and leverage that power to *impact* others. "To thine own self be true" (Hamlet 1.3.78). Be true to yourself and others will follow.

—Anonymous

Dear Lilly,

George Burns said, "The key to success is sincerity. If you can fake that, you've got it made."

Remember early in your career when your wife sat down with you and said, "They are about to throw you out of the Dale Carnegie class you are taking." She was one of the instructors and was going to be one of the votes to remove you from the class!

"How is that possible?" you asked, "I aced every talk and took home the pen, and the Lincoln biography." These were the treasured prizes you won for masterful storytelling in the preceding weeks.

She shook her head, "Absolutely correct, you were the top speaker every week. But in the instructor meeting, we all realized that none of the stories you were telling said anything about you. They were perfect at winning, but this isn't a public speaking contest. It is supposed to be about you building a genuine connection with your audience."

As a career negotiator, public speaking champion, even radio personality—your successes were all built upon years of sounding sincere. But a childhood of hiding your thoughts and feelings from savagely critical parents led you to build a social persona: a mask that was impenetrable (except to some of the most perceptive coaches in the world, and it still took them seven weeks to figure us out).

To this day, I am still not 100% sure my wife didn't rat us out to them!

You had never been asked to leave a program like that before. Sure, you were fired from being an altar boy—but that is another letter.

So the next class, you dug deep to tell a moving and heartfelt story. One that showed a lot about us, opened up, displayed vulnerability. You didn't win the competition that week, but that was no longer the objective. That story kept you in the program to graduate.

This experience has now become even more valuable in today's exploding AI-driven world.

Because it happened decades before vulnerability was "discovered" and ruthlessly monetized.

There is now an entire industry devoted to faking sincerity.

Today, AI is capable of creating far more content than humans—factual and otherwise. It can hit every beat, follow the frameworks perfectly, and tell heartwarming stories. As a result, genuineness and sincerity are becoming the currencies for humans competing in this new world.

Technology will tell the perfect story, checking all of the boxes and winning every prize. But we are entering the stage of the technology usually called the "uncanny valley." This term comes from animation, when it became technically perfect, and yet audiences could still sense that it was fake. Uncanny.

AI is now good enough to achieve that objective perfection, and it gets better every month. It is always going to win the prize for that perfection. So real stories imperfectly told are now the critical skill for leaders, and humans.

So Lilly, the prize isn't about the perfect delivery anymore, not even for the perfect content; the prize is the connection we make by being truly sincere—not faking it.

Stephen

Stephen Sopko
USA
linkedin.com/in/stephensopko

Dear Lilly,

I am a survivor of physical, emotional, and financial abuse.

It happened during my marriage.

I have never written about it before. Some of the things I'm going to tell you I have never shared with anyone except my therapist.

When I was 18, I went travelling far from home. I wanted an adventure!

There I met a seemingly lovely young man, also 18, traveling and from my home country.

After returning home, although living in different cities, we officially started dating. Five years later and post college degrees, we got married.

We were both 23.

Getting married straight after college was widespread at the time. It was just what everyone did.

Throughout our marriage, I experienced traumatic abuse. I wondered if it was what being married was like. It's just that no one had told me.

He used to rage at me.

He would shout and lose his temper over the smallest of things.

He used to beat me hard, with his fists.

I did the best I could to protect myself, especially my face and head, but the bruises on my upper body and legs told their own story.

Late at night, I would lock myself into the bathroom to try and protect myself, but he would lever open the door and continue dragging and beating me even though I screamed and begged him to stop.

He didn't.

I wondered if the neighbors could hear me screaming.

He would say, "I've never used my full strength," and "You've never ended up in hospital, so what are you making such a fuss about?'

He would poke me at night to stop me from sleeping and pull off the duvet from our shared bed even when the weather was cold. He belittled me.

I was bewildered, wretched, ashamed, and depressed, constantly walking on eggshells, second guessing what he might do and piling on weight. I believed it was my fault.

Domestic abuse was not acknowledged as being a society-wide issue at that time, though it was and still is.

Two things then happened, which enabled me to understand what was going on and what I might choose to do next.

I was working in a psychiatric provision for children who had experienced appalling abuse at the hands of their parents. For the first time, because of the behavior of one child towards a member of staff, I understood what projective identification was. I realized that my relationship with my husband had the same dynamic. He couldn't process his feelings as an adult and didn't take responsibility for his behavior. He accused <u>me</u> of all the behaviors that he was demonstrating. This realization was liberating.

Then I picked up a book written for women in abusive relationships. The key message was to challenge the behaviors and say: "if you don't stop, I will leave." The challenge was terrifying, but I said it.

He didn't stop, so I left.

Many people around me at the time DIDN'T believe me, including some of my closest friends. That multiplied the trauma.

Since then, I have chosen a journey of healing, which has been balm to my heart and soul. I wish I had space to tell you more. This is enough for now.

A survivor.

Mia Campbell
United Kingdom

Dear Lilly,

I know this time in your life feels confusing and uncertain. You're being asked to make big decisions about your future—about who you want to be—before you've even had the chance to really live it. People see your confidence, your voice, your spark, and they nudge you toward broadcast journalism. They mean well. They love you. And you want to make them proud.

Those first couple of years in college feel fine, but by junior year, reality starts knocking. You take that internship at the local TV station, full of hope and excitement, ready to learn. But the world you step into is nothing like you imagined. The newsroom is loud, fast, and harsh. You get treated like a barista more often than a journalist. The language, the cynicism... it wears on you.

There's one bright light, though: a kind videographer who believes in you and takes the time to help you grow. You'll remember his encouragement for years to come.

But even with that, you start to feel it deep down: *This isn't where I belong.*

You tell your parents you don't think this is the right path, but they remind you to finish what you started. So you do. You work hard, earn that degree, and walk proudly across the graduation stage. You celebrate, even though something inside you already knows this isn't your forever.

Less than a year later, you move four hours from home for your first "dream job." You're making $18,000 a year, working multiple side jobs just to keep the lights on. You barely sleep, and no matter how hard you try, you don't feel fulfilled. Everyone says, "Just put in a few years. Work your way up. You'll make it." But deep down, you know better.

Four years later, when you're standing there with a microphone in someone's face during one of the hardest moments of their life, your heart whispers again: *This isn't it.* And this time, you listen. The stress, the pressure, even your health—your body starts showing you what your spirit's been saying all along.

Here's the thing to remember: Don't be angry at the people who guided you here. They loved you and wanted the best for you. They saw your gifts before you did. But learning how to use those gifts in a way that brings joy and peace—that's something only you and the Lord can figure out together.

Looking back, I can see that even this season had purpose. God used it to shape you, to teach you, to prepare you for what was next.

Now I know how important joy and fulfillment are in your work, and how crucial it is to pay attention when something doesn't feel right. Find what you love and do what lights you up! Because when you don't, your health, happiness, relationships, and future all pay the price.

And yes—thankfully, you won't have high blood pressure anymore, now that you're doing what you love.

Love,
Kate

Kate Bays
USA
https://www.linkedin.com/in/katebays/

Dear Jodi,

When I was growing up, I had very few resources. My parents got married when they were 17 and 23. By the time they had me, their fourth child, things were really tight. Our bread and treats were from the day-old bin. For Christmas, we got necessities: socks, underwear, umbrellas. In the winter, I remember standing over a heat register to get warm and, in the summer, we stayed in the one room with air conditioning, and placed sheets in the doorways to keep the coldness in. My parents did their best and they taught me good manners, a strong work ethic, and to be brave.

The challenge started when I began dreaming of a different life. I put pen to paper and wrote about exotic places, shelves of books, and exciting careers. These were foreign concepts to my parents who did not graduate from eighth grade or travel, so I immediately felt different. An outlier. I never felt like I belonged anywhere and felt both guilty and sad about these feelings. I had no idea why they did not want the same things. I had no idea why I wanted a different life.

After college, my best friend April and I hopped into my tiny red Mazda RX 7 with no air and traveled from Pennsylvania to Colorado. It was the first time my soul felt free. I was in awe of the various majestic landscapes, loved the challenge of the stubborn paper map which refused order, and the other travelers, who like us, were curious and diverted by each approaching landmark. It was a trip of a lifetime, and the next time I did something so spectacular was soon after my young husband Kevin was diagnosed with ALS at the age of 30.

For a very long time, I allowed myself to feel less than. I did not feel worthy of anything. I did not allow myself to think of things that cost money: traveling outside of the U.S., taking classes, matching furniture.

When my husband Kevin battled ALS, it was an awakening of many things. My enormous commitment to his journey and quality of life, the impact it had on our young daughter Alina, that life is short. My brother Jamie sent us to Bermuda. Kevin loved to swim and snorkel. I remember sitting on Horseshoe Bay beach, shades hiding tears, as his body refused to cooperate. I was torn between the beauty of the island and the reality of his terminal illness.

In 2001, when Kevin, 36 years old, passed away, I was a shell of my former self. I was exhausted, depressed, and clueless about any dreams. My dreams died with him.

It is clear that one thing saved me: purpose. I started to work at the ALS Hope Foundation and continued my advocacy and leadership work in the ALS world. I met another family who loved and lost because of ALS and we became one. I became a bonus mom to two children, Nora and Adam, and a wife again. My husband Benton and I started a non-profit, Hope Loves Company, which was born out of our combined losses. Today, Hope Loves Company brings free resources to children and teens across the U.S. who love someone or have lost someone to ALS.

I feel so much love for my younger self. I feel so much pain for her too. She had no idea that her skills and gifts were too bright for living small. She felt lost, alone, sad, and different for more than four decades. That's a long time to not love who you are. I am reminded of the poem, which was my high school yearbook quote by R.L. Sharpe:

Each is given a bag of tools,
A shapeless mass,
A book of rules;
And each must make—

Ere life is flown—
A stumbling block
Or a steppingstone.

That little girl who felt alone is no more. She made it!
Jodi

Jodi O'Donnell Ames
USA
https://www.linkedin.com/in/jodi-o-donnell-ames-8b955a40/

Dear Lilly,

There are moments in life when starting again is not a choice—it's survival.

I left Kenya after a painful separation from my husband of 16 years. I had to leave behind my three sons, our shared dreams, and everything we had built together. Our culture made it difficult for me to take the children, and the heartbreak of leaving them behind was heavier than the single suitcase I carried. With just one hundred dollars and a trembling hope, I relocated to America to rebuild my life from scratch.

At first, it felt like my world had ended. But in the quiet of uncertainty, I found purpose. I began serving in American-led churches, where I learned the power of structure, excellence, and leadership grounded in integrity. Later, I began sharing what I had learned with immigrant-led churches—helping them build systems, empower volunteers, and lead with vision.

That's where I discovered my leadership voice. I realized leadership isn't about titles or applause; it's about service, stewardship, and transformation. Each act of service became a healing process that restored not only my confidence but also my calling.

After ten years in the U.S., I returned to Kenya to bury my mother—and I never went back. Upon returning, people began to ask me for jobs. But as I listened to their stories, I realized they weren't really looking for employment; they were searching for fulfillment. That insight birthed PassionProfit, a leadership and enterprise development company that helps individuals and organizations discover their purpose, design pathways for impact, and foster the creation of decent work across Africa and beyond.

Today, I am the author of Authentic Leadership: A Playbook to Discover Who You Are, Design Ecosystems that Harmonize Callings, and Drive Significance.

Looking back, I see that starting again wasn't the end. It was the turning point. Every loss stripped away what was temporary so that what was eternal could emerge. I left Kenya broken, but I returned whole—with purpose, vision, and a renewed passion to help others rise again too.

With love and grace,
Frida Owinga

Frida Owinga
Kenya
https://www.linkedin.com/in/fridaowinga/

Dear Little Man,

Hey… look at you.

Seven years old, barefoot, a little dirt on your cheek, that wild grin that can't hide how much you already want to be somebody.

You don't know it yet, but you already are.

I see how hard you're trying to be brave. I see how you puff your chest out, how you tell stories to make people laugh, how you want everyone to think you're tough.

I know the real reason you do it. You just don't want to feel invisible.

You won't always understand why you don't fit in. You'll watch other kids seem to have it all figured out, and you'll start wondering what's wrong with you.

But there's nothing wrong with you, kid. You're just different, and one day, that difference will become your superpower.

You've got this big heart you keep trying to hide. Don't.

That heart will save lives one day, including your own.

You're going to grow up and build something massive. You'll start a company, and it'll be your greatest teacher.

It's going to strip you down, make you question everything, and it will hurt. It'll knock you flat on your knees. You'll lose sleep, lose people, and lose parts of yourself you thought you needed.

But what's left standing... is gold. Pure, unshakable gold.

Like Ponyboy watching that sunrise and realizing there's still beauty after the chaos.

You'll love people hard. You'll lose some. You'll learn that walls don't protect you, they just keep love out. So let people in, even when it's scary. Especially when it's scary.

And that girl you're going to meet?

Oh man, she's everything. She's fire and grace all rolled together. She's going to see through all your walls, all your bullshit, all your noise, and love you anyway.

She'll be your mirror when you forget who you are.

Don't ever take her for granted. She's the reason you stay grounded when the world starts spinning too fast.

And one day, you'll look around at the life you built, the people you've lifted up, the stories you've lived, the man you've become... and you'll realize something powerful.

All that pain, all that confusion, all those lonely nights... they were never punishment.

They were preparation.

You'll finally understand that every time you fell, every time you doubted yourself, it was shaping you into someone who could turn struggle into purpose.

So here's what I want you to remember, little man:

You don't have to be the toughest.
You don't have to be the loudest.
You just have to keep being you.

That's enough. It always was.

Come here…

Fist bump.

I'm proud of you, kid.
You made it.

And damn, what a ride it's been.
Donnie

Donnie Boivin
USA
https://www.linkedin.com/in/donnieboivin

Dear Lilly,

Leadership isn't just about guiding others—it's about knowing when to pause, reflect, and receive. For years, I showed up strong, steady, and full of grace, always ready to pour into others. I thought being a leader meant never asking for help, never showing cracks. Turns out, that's not leadership—that's exhaustion with a fancy title.

In February 2025, I rang the bell. Not just any bell, but the kind that says, "You made it through." That moment didn't just close a chapter; it opened a floodgate of blessings and opportunities. Since then, life has been serving up abundance like it's on a mission. New doors opened, old fears faded, and I've been reminded daily that grace has a way of circling back—especially when you've spent years "paying into it."

One of the biggest lessons? Asking for help isn't weakness—it's wisdom. For someone who prided herself on being the go-to, the fixer, the "I've got it" person, learning to say "I need support" was humbling. But also freeing. And let's be honest—sometimes the strongest move is letting someone else carry the heavy grocery bags while you hold the ice cream.

Loving yourself means celebrating your wins (even the small ones, like not replying to that email at midnight), embracing your scars (physical and emotional), and letting people walk beside you—even when you're used to leading the parade. It's realizing that leadership isn't about being perfect; it's about being real. And when you lead from a place of self-love, you give others permission to do the same.

Today, I lead with a lighter heart and a deeper laugh. I bring grace, humility, and a whole lot of gratitude into every room I enter. I know now that the most powerful leaders aren't the ones who never fall; they're the ones who rise, again and again, with love in their hearts and maybe a little glitter on their shoes.

Magda

Magda DeMauro
USA
https://www.linkedin.com/in/magda-demauro-4a11b613a/

Dear Lilly,

When I first started my job as a Comms Exec many, many years ago, one of my biggest challenges was working with the design team. Designers are naturally creative—they have strong ideas, bold visions, and a passion for originality. On the other hand, my role was to guide—ensuring that our materials aligned with what management wanted—often more formal, structured, and brand-consistent.

At first, this difference in perspective caused tension. The designer felt restricted by corporate guidelines, while I grew frustrated that he didn't seem to understand the practical expectations from our bosses. We went back and forth, voicing opinion upon opinion, but the designer still did not budge. Eventually, I reached my limit. In a moment of frustration, I blew my top, and it escalated into a shouting match, something I had never imagined happening.

Afterwards, I went to the washroom and had a good cry. The pressure of managing that one person, balancing expectations from both sides, and trying to keep everything on track became overwhelming. I felt like I had failed, both as a communicator and as a team lead.

But that difficult moment became a turning point. I realized that leadership isn't about controlling others— it's about managing emotions, listening deeply, and finding calm even in conflict. The next day, I apologized to the designer and asked for a fresh start. This time, I approached the discussion with empathy, acknowledging his creative needs while clearly explaining our corporate goals. Slowly, we began to understand each other's perspectives and eventually found middle ground, producing designs that satisfied both creativity and compliance.

Things started to improve. Our working relationship grew stronger. We developed a deeper understanding and mutual respect, and what once was a source of tension became one of genuine collaboration. We truly enjoyed working together—bouncing ideas off one another and celebrating each successful project as a shared victory.

Three years flew by, and then he decided to resign to start his own design company. I was ecstatic for him—proud to see him take that bold step to pursue his passion. But not long after, tragic news came. He had passed away due to the immense pressure of managing his own business; it had simply become too much for him.

Till this day, I still recall fondly how our working relationship began—rocky, emotional, and full of lessons. From that experience, I learned that leadership is not just about guiding people toward goals but about understanding them as human beings. It's about patience, compassion, and humility—because sometimes, the greatest connections and lessons come from the most difficult beginnings.

And I will always remember him—Ismadi—for teaching me that lesson.

Syarina

Syarina Mohd Idris
Malaysia
https://www.linkedin.com/in/syarina-mohd-idris-6754ab31/

Dear Little Zack,

I have so much to be grateful for because of you. You have allowed life experiences to shape you so that you are able to unconditionally love, care, and respect life and all it gives you.

As you cross the border from Canada into the great U. S., with your family and meager possessions tightly packed into a newly purchased, pinehurst green Oldsmobile Delta 88, your life experiences *really* start and will *not* stop. Thankfully.

You just left your birthplace that you called home for 10 years. The emotions of excitement, happiness, fear, and discomfort are all vying for your attention. Traveling to a "foreign" land with your eyes and ears wide open, you will begin at lightning speed to absorb everything your young sensory systems can handle, storing it into bottomless buckets for future use. You will take in your parents' brave journey facing the trials and tribulations of a new country that did not necessarily invite them. You watch as they tirelessly care and provide for a family, barely speaking the native language and having no lifeline nearby, all for a chance at a better opportunity. This will feed your own curiosity and resilience to try new things with courage you did not know you have. You, with your own young family, will move seven times, for a chance at a better opportunity, carrying with you those all too familiar emotions of excitement, fear, happiness, and discomfort.

At age 13, working in the restaurant your parents sacrificed to start, you will see, hear, and feel things you have never experienced before. Taking risks. Pride. The importance of quality and customer satisfaction. Running a business and not letting it run you. Mistakes. Failures. Toxicity. Loyalty. Treating customers and employees with empathy. And especially this: watching your father treat an employee with kindness after catching her stealing will shape your point of view and ability to treat people like humans. This will eternally guide you.

You will meet a 16-year old girl weighing only 40 pounds because of her debilitating disease, while you yourself are an immature boy of 17 and 270 pounds. You will become best friends. You learn to start overcoming that persistent and pestering lack of confidence, growing your self-awareness and emotional confidence, and you will learn how to deeply love and care for another human. You will never ever complain that life is that hard again. Even after her death at 25, you will carry with you her legacy of love, kindness, respect, and understanding.

You will meet and marry your soulmate, a person who doesn't just make you a better person but teaches you about the importance of loving and respecting each other first and foremost, and the rest, like raising a good family, falls into place.

Through trials and tribulations, even still at 63 years young, you will tap into the life experiences that began at 10. I thank you and love you from the bottom of my heart for being you.

Zack

Zack Demopoulos
USA
https://www.linkedin.com/in/zackdemopoulos/

Dear Lilly,

If I could sit across from my younger invisible self, I'd start with a deep breath and a smile that says, *"You don't have to keep running so hard, baby."*

You've been carrying so much: expectations, responsibility, and the belief that if you just work harder, love harder, give more, everything will fall into place. We lived that story for a long time.

I thought exhaustion meant I was doing something right. That the more I poured out, the more worthy I'd be.

But what I've learned over time is this: Being tired all the time isn't strength. It's a sign. And if you don't stop and listen to it, your body and your spirit will do it for you.

I used to think leadership was about showing up for everyone else. But we ended up learning that it starts with showing up for ourselves, the quiet kind of leadership that happens when we stop pretending we're fine and admit what's really going on inside our brains.

It was a hard lesson, but we know now that you can't lead from an empty place. You can't love others deeply if you've forgotten how to love yourself.

So, here's what I want you to remember:

- Pause.
- Take inventory—not of your to-do list, but of your heart.
- Ask yourself, *What am I feeling? Why? And what do I need right now?*

Those questions will save you more times than you know.

I wish you could see how peace changes everything. How rest doesn't make you lazy; it makes you powerful. How saying "no" sometimes means saying "yes" to your own well-being.

And most of all, I wish you'd stop trying to prove yourself. You already are enough, not because of what you do, but because of who you are.

So, the next time life feels heavy, take that deep breath. Look yourself in the mirror. Check in: not as a boss, not as a mother, not as a friend, but as a woman who's still learning, still growing, still worthy.

That's the real "check-up from the neck-up."

It's just you, getting honest with yourself, and giving yourself the love you've been giving everyone else.

Priscilla J. Murphy
USA
https://www.linkedin.com/in/priscillamurphy/

Dear Lilly,

Fear has a way of pretending it's bigger than it is.

When you're little, it shows up quietly in your stomach before a performance, or in your throat when everyone's eyes are on you. I remember being six, dressed for a solo dance performance on stage, ready to dance: until I saw hundreds of faces staring back. My body froze and I left without performing. I sat at the back of the stage crying, and that moment stayed with me for years.

But here's what you'll learn: Fear shrinks when you face it.

You'll start small: performing in groups, then slowly stepping into the lead. Each time, fear will whisper, *"What if you fail?"* And each time, you'll show up anyway. And one day, you'll stand in front of hundreds, speaking with confidence and joy. The same stage that once terrified you will become your home.

It doesn't stop there. Fear will follow you into adulthood too, disguised in different forms. Like when you're on a plane, your palms sweating, with that feeling that you will throw up any minute, certain that flying isn't for you. So, you'll do something wild: take a consulting job that requires flying every week—Monday mornings and Thursday evenings in the air. You'll get queasy, then you'll get stronger, and eventually you'll look out the window at the clouds and smile, realizing you've reclaimed the sky.

Courage, you'll learn, isn't about not being afraid; it's about walking straight toward what scares you, one step at a time.

And when doubt creeps in, when you start to wonder if you're "ready" or "good enough," remember this: Fear feeds on avoidance. The moment you look it in the eye, it starts to lose its power.

One day, you'll see fear for what it really is: a sign that you're growing. You'll learn to thank it, not run from it. You'll make a habit of choosing the harder path, not because it's easy, but because it's where courage lives.

So, dear Lilly, the next time your hands tremble before a big moment, don't shrink back. Take a breath. Step forward anyway. The world belongs to the women who face what frightens them, and you are becoming one of them.

With Love,
Uvika

Uvika Sharma
USA
https://www.linkedin.com/in/uvika-sharma/

Dear Lilly,

One of my favorite birds is the Barred Owl. When I am on a walk at dusk and see a

Barred Owl fly low through the woods, my breath catches, and I stand completely still. I am amazed by the size and beauty of the owl. I am grateful for the experience of standing still and being completely in the present moment while in the presence of this beautiful bird.

A life experience I practice and suggest to you is to stand completely still one time every day. Ask yourself: "What do I love at this moment?" This practice gives me the chance every day to feel love and connection to nature, a person, or my sweet dog Murphy. My wish for you is to have a similar daily connection as a way to feel connected and a sense of love.

To help you remember this practice, I created an acronym for you.

O.W.L. This means Observe, Wait, and Love.

How long do I suggest that you O.W. L.? That's up to you. One slow inhale and one slow exhale might be just the right amount of time. Pick the length of time that fits you. Do you have to be outside on a walk? You can be anywhere you want. Inside. Outside. By yourself. With someone. With a pet. Do you have to do this every day? That's up to you.

It's okay to get thrown off and then start up again with your O.W.L. practice. Because I am older now, I want you to know about this practice. I started this practice when my daughter was a baby. She's all grown up now. My days go by really fast. My wish for you is to have an O.W.L. experience every day as a way to love others, love your life, love yourself, and to not feel alone.

Gotta go! It's dusk outside and I want to be available in case the Barred Owl flies by and gives me an opportunity to O.W.L.

XOXO
Dawn

Dawn Carney-Meriwether
USA
https://www.linkedin.com/in/dawn-carney-meriwether-pcc-63b466b6/

Dear Lilly,

I know 15 feels hard. That ache of hollowness that you feel. It's real. And I wish I could tell you that it was going to go away, but it's not.

You snuck out of your house once to go to a party, held a wine cooler in your hand for an hour, nursed it, and didn't see the point of people being stupid and out of control.

At that party, you just wanted someone to talk to.
Someone to see you.
Someone to validate that you were worth connecting with.

You've been told since childhood that marriage is the answer. What makes you complete.

And so you crave human companionship that is equal to the fantasy that you make marriage out to be.

The schism between your dad's interpretation of spirituality
And the behaviors that were required
Have put a deep wondering about what it takes to earn love
You love him more than anything
But everything according to him is "worldly" and "fleshly"
Especially relationships. Oh the relationships.

It's like they're straight from the fires of hell.

"Beware of the Lust of the Flesh. It moves like a roaring, caged animal. Don't let it out lest you be swallowed in its fury."

Relationships are forbidden, scary,

But so damn tantalizing.

And then shame… The shame kicks in.

So you turn into the good kid.
The good kid who pushes it all down. You push it all down.

And start to be the person others need so that they can solve their problems

Your problems don't matter. You can fix your problems by solving others' problems.

Sweet thing.

It's going to take an affair in your adult life.

A six-month "best sex of your life" affair—a mind-altering, integrity-challenging, red-flag-waving, volcano-exploding, separation-inducing, hollowness-evoking, addiction-questioning, "Who the hell am I" wondering affair…

An affair that you will eventually learn was a mask for what you thought you needed. When what you really needed was to discover that no *one* person's validation, (despite the mind-blowing sex), will ever make you feel whole.

Now here you are. You know what you do with that hollowness now at 45?
You lean into it. And remind yourself.

You are enough.
You will always be enough.
You are in the process of discovering that enoughness.

The hollow will never be filled by another.

And you kind of like cursing now. Just sayin'

No one can know the best version of you that you've been given until you let it emerge from underneath all that curiosity-inducing feeling…

You used to call it shame.

Now you label it and ask what it is that YOU need. And you thank it.
Good for you.

You, my friend, my sweet friend, have an ever-increasing capacity to create space for the most important person in your life.

And the people you touch in life will *feel* the space you've created.

And that will liberate them to create the space they need for themselves.

You're a beautiful soul.
You.
Yes, You.
Keep leaning in.

With all the love that is yet to be experienced from all the places that are deepest within your own soul,

Your future self

(Anonymous)

Dear Lilly,

I know you've always prided yourself on being strong, capable, and independent. You've worn resilience like armor and convinced yourself that asking for help somehow means you're not enough.

You know what? That's crap! It's OK to ask for help.

You don't have to go it alone.

There will be moments when the weight feels heavy, really heavy; when the expectations, the goals, and the noise around you make it hard to breathe. In those moments, look around. You'll find people standing quietly on the sidelines, ready to step in. They see your potential, even when you doubt it. They want to help you rise, not because they think you can't do it alone, but because they know we're all stronger together.

Asking for help doesn't make you weaker. It makes you wiser. It opens doors to curiosity, to learning, connection, and grace. It creates space for others to bring their light to your path, just as you will one day do for them.

You already have everything you need within you: your PHEAR Advantage!

Use it. Every day.

Let your **Purpose** guide you, your **Heart** ground you, your **Energy** sustain you, your **Action** move you, and your **Reflection** remind you how far you've come.

You are not meant to be everything for everyone. You are meant to be you—the best version of yourself: evolving, growing, and becoming.

So, the next time you feel like you must handle it all, pause. Take a breath. Ask for help. You'll be amazed at who shows up and how much lighter the journey feels when you let others walk beside you.

Always on (and by) your side,
Suha

Suha Beidas Zehl
USA
https://www.linkedin.com/in/suhabeidaszehl/

Dear Lilly,

"Freedom is not free. It is always purchased with the high price of sacrifice and suffering." - Rev. Dr. Martin L. King, Jr.

As a young girl, it was easy to take freedom for granted. You went to school at a time when the only "drill" you were participating in was a fire drill. You played with your friends, went to church, and lived in a neighborhood untouched by even the threat of war.

Yes, you knew veterans and had family members who served in the Vietnam War, but they never talked about it. It became a history lesson taught in school without real understanding of the sacrifices, the loss, the trauma, the extended sickness, and the overall horrors of war. You were shielded from understanding what the real cost of freedom was (and still is).

However, when you begin working for the government, you work alongside colleagues from all branches of the military. You meet both veterans and active-duty service men and women and continue to be impressed by their stories and in awe of their service. You also begin to understand that "service to country" isn't limited solely to service members. Service becomes both an honor and a sacrifice that the entire family makes every day, in the name of freedom.

The toll of service impacts everyone: from the servicemember, to their spouse, to their children, to their extended families. From deployments to full family moves, the constant threat of war somewhere in the world, fear of whether their loved one will come home, serving when one may not fully understand or align with the mission… the list is long and burdensome. Yet you never hear them complain.

Your history books in school never taught the full toll that comes with the price of freedom. As an adult you will begin visiting presidential libraries (from both parties), and you will begin taking opportunities to learn more about the wars that have impacted the freedom you mistakenly once took for granted.

Ronald Reagan said, "Freedom is a fragile thing and is never more than one generation away from extinction. It is ours by inheritance; it must be fought for and defended constantly by each generation."

Lesson in Leadership & Loving Yourself: Just as you work to understand your business, continue to educate yourself on the price of freedom, especially today. It really does impact everything: from economies, to businesses, to school drills. It is so easy to take such an amazing gift for granted. And while the need for self-care and loving yourself remains an important daily practice, take the time to thank a veteran or active military personnel.

They deserve to know that they too are loved and appreciated for a gift we will never be able to repay.

With love always,
Ali

Dear Lilly,

First things first—you're not behind. I know it feels like you should've arrived by now. Like there's a checklist you forgot to print. But there isn't. There's just you, your pace, and a life that gets built one brave decision at a time.

Leadership won't always look the way you expect it to. It won't always come with titles or applause. Sometimes, it looks like staying calm when everyone else is spiraling. Sometimes, it's knowing when to speak—and when to listen. And sometimes, it's just keeping your standards when it would be easier to cut corners.

You don't have to be the loudest person in the room to be heard. Just be clear. Be steady. Be you. That's more powerful than you think.

And while we're being honest, don't wait until you feel "ready" to start something. Ready is a myth. Most of the time, you just learn by doing. And by messing up. And by doing it again, but with more experience and snacks.

Your value isn't how perfectly you perform—it's how consistently you *show up*. With clarity. With integrity. With a little humor. And maybe a backup plan, because, well… cool tech is great when it works, but sometimes, it doesn't.

You're not lost. You're becoming. And that's exactly where you're supposed to be.

With Love (and strong coffee),
Bernie – aka "Mr. Mustache"

Bernie DeSantis III
USA
https://www.linkedin.com/in/badiii/

Dear Lilly,

I grew up as a minister's daughter, the eldest sibling to two deaf brothers, and I learned at a very young age, "You have to be strong." Bullies were rampant then. There was no "anti-bullying" campaign to save us. I remember being bullied and seeing the bully taking great pleasure in my discomfort. The bullies had the upper hand, until I learned to be a fighter, a champion for myself and others.

I prefaced this so that you can understand that when I went into the workplace, I thought, "At last, people would be adults." *Boy,* did I have a rude awakening. Bullying existed but was much more subversive and more indirect in its presentation than my childhood experiences.

Eight years into a retail management career, I worked hard and went to college while working 50+ hours a week. I advanced quickly and learned enough to train the new store managers coming into the company. Then one day, I thought, I'm training—specifically, men—to do the job.

So I threw my hat in the ring. Oh, the flattery they threw my way: "You're so smart, talented, quick to learn new processes, a great teacher." But it was gratuitous flattery, not genuine. They would say, "You're too young for this position," and they took pleasure in my discomfort. My work ethic benefited their agenda—I was young, inexperienced in the politics of the workplace. So I held on for another five years, doing the same and more, all while not being promoted. Enough was enough. I quit and moved on.

My life lesson was: Don't confuse backhanded flattery as true appreciation of your talent. True appreciation in the workplace includes opportunities for promotions and pay raises. Otherwise, it is a form of bullying, a way to hold you back and hold you down. No one should try to make you feel "less than." Throughout my life, many have tried to make me feel poorly (and many have succeeded), but I have come to learn it was *them* trying to feel better about themselves and had nothing to do with my self-worth. And while I still have "imposter syndrome," feeling like any minute now the bottom will fall through and the "truth" of my inadequacy will be known to all, I'm learning every day: I am worthy, and it *is* my hard work that has brought me this far.

My lesson in leadership is: Don't be the one to give backhanded compliments or hold a good staff member back because they benefit you. Be genuine with your staff; honesty and forthrightness will build a strong foundation for your team. As a champion of their hard work, your words of encouragement will go places that a dollar bill will not.

I hope this resonates with you, and you find that champion in yourself and for your teams.

Warm regards,
Debbie

Deborah LaBonte
USA
https://www.linkedin.com/in/deborah-labonte-88091676/

Dear Lilly,

The girl in the broken crib.

The girl in this photo was curious, creative, and mischievous. Don't be fooled, she still is.

Somehow her existence infuriated her mother. Nothing she did was ever enough to impress.

One of her earliest memories: being pinned down by the arms and force-fed amoxicillin.

Then her brother was born, and he was an angel. So she became more of an annoyance. Too much for a parent who had no patience.

Her cute curly hair was her greatest asset, the only thing people stopped and admired. According to a world that valued a different kind of beauty, her quirky personality wasn't as attractive.

She didn't understand why she was unlikeable. So she was destined to become a high-achieving people pleaser.

She excelled academically. Writing, reading, sports captain. Played violin and guitar. Won a national poetry competition, published by 11. Editor of the school newspaper.

But her curiosity? That was an issue. Apparently, an attitude problem. Asking questions became an act of rebellion. Every school report "noted" it.

Not a child on a quest to understand the world. An empath and undiagnosed neurodivergent triggered by injustice.

Still, she couldn't impress the person whose love and admiration she coveted. By now, her sass was a bigger problem. She was "just like her dad," apparently a bad thing.

This triggered the one who constantly reminded her she was a disappointment. Not as good as her friends, whose achievements her mum celebrated endlessly.

So she worked harder. Tried more. Went into healthcare. Studied pharmacy. A career helping people; that's worthy, surely?

Away at college, her parents split up. Her dad was broken, and it hurt to see him suffer. The relationship with her mother got tougher, but she didn't give up. Family—you don't get to stop trying.

By this point, she was conflicted. Popular at uni. Made friends easily. Earning money. Successful on paper. Ticking all the "perfect daughter" boxes.

But she'd started to believe she wasn't worthy of love. Self-worth on the floor. Value based on what she did, not who she was at soul level.

There's no blame here. But there's a pattern.

Children who grow up being told they aren't worthy end up in toxic relationships. Friendship circles where they exist on the edge. Careers where they're exceptional at their profession but still annoying people simply by existing.

Because they've spent their whole lives seeking external validation. Making people around them happy, knowing they aren't really wanted.

They don't learn healthy boundaries. They inherit limiting beliefs. Imposter stories. They learn to project confidence and lead with purpose while drowning inside.

It wasn't until her forties, after she'd finally realised living in fear wasn't normal and left her abusive partner, that she discovered not everyone's behind-closed-doors life involved walking on eggshells.

She joined a group with other survivors. Learned about narcissistic personality disorders. Realised not every family existed like that. But the behaviours she learned growing up? That's what shaped her reality.

She hadn't known better. But now she did.

She understood that for some people, she would never fit the criteria. Never make them happy. And she could finally start her new chapter.

She thought domestic abuse was "being hit by your partner."

She didn't know it was how a parent treated you. Words and belittling actions. Watching abuse thrive in the home you grew up in.

She isn't writing this for pity. She's writing to raise awareness of how an educated woman can end up in this situation, oblivious, because it's not on the education curriculum.

The dad she was "too like"? He adores her. He's her best friend. He too was a victim. He might not have physical bruises, but he has the mental scars.

And she was blessed with resilience and inner knowing that she would finally find her path.

That girl is me.

Rachael Lemon
England
https://www.linkedin.com/in/rachaellemon-leadership-coach-mentor/

Dear Lilly,

If I could sit with you for just a moment—maybe over coffee, before another long day of trying to prove yourself—I would tell you something that will take you years to believe:

You do not need to be perfect to be powerful.

You have been taught that leadership means always having the answers, holding it together, smiling when your heart is heavy. But real leadership, the kind that changes rooms, companies, and lives, begins the moment you allow yourself to be real.

Courage is not loud, Lilly. It does not always roar in the boardroom or stride across stages. Sometimes it is quiet, like showing up when you feel unseen, or saying, "I do not know" when you are expected to have every solution. Courage is choosing to keep your heart open when experience tells you to close it.

You will fail too: spectacularly, publicly, sometimes painfully. But those moments will not define you; they will refine you. Every disappointment will shape the compassion you one day give others. Every time you fall, you will learn that resilience is not about bouncing back; it is about rising differently.

And self-belief? That is the hardest one.

You will have seasons where you lose it entirely. You will doubt your worth, your work, your place in the room. But every time you rebuild it, it will come back stronger—shaped by evidence, not ego. You will learn that believing in yourself is not arrogance; it is self-respect.

So, lead gently—with others and with yourself. Speak kindly to the woman in the mirror. Rest when you need to. Trust that your softness will never make you small.

Because one day, people will look to you not because you were fearless, but because you were authentic.

And that will be your greatest strength of all.

With love,
Corina

Corina Goetz
London, UK

Dear Little Nadine,

You don't need to prove yourself so much.

I know you think you do. You think if you just work harder, say yes more often, stay late a few more nights... people will notice. They'll see your worth.

But your worth isn't something you earn. It's something you already have. You just haven't learned to trust it yet. You have not yet shown people how great the real you is.

You may spend years chasing the idea of perfection: the title, the role that seems best, or the ideal version of yourself. You'll measure success in promotions, praise, titles, and salary. And for a while, that will feel good. You'll think that's what leadership looks like.

But one day, you'll hit a crossroads where you realize that does not make you happy. Leadership isn't about having the title, or even the best answers. Maybe leadership is not really what you thought you wanted; it's actually connection with others, and them seeing you as a connector. It's a leader through a new lens. You will find your true strengths in the most unlikely place— people you meet through online communities and social networks like LinkedIn.

You'll learn that vulnerability isn't weakness. It's the doorway to connection. It's the gold cracks that need to be celebrated (Kintsugi), and it's the journey along the way… not always the destination.

You will develop gratitude as more than a practice. It will be something that lives and breathes within you each day. It's true active appreciation that you will share, and create a ripple effect of kindness. You will lean into gratitude to help you, especially when things feel uncertain.

You'll have moments where you feel lost or behind. You'll wonder if you're doing enough, giving enough, *being* enough.

And I want you to know, you are. You always were. Your daughter is too. You will try to teach her all of this, and she is 14, so she won't listen. But someday, she will.

It's all a journey: for you, for her, as a human, as a mom… Every stumble taught you something. Every detour shaped your resilience.

Every person who believed in you saw something you couldn't yet see in yourself.

One day, you'll stop apologizing for being too much, too talkative, too passionate, too emotional, too opinionated, etc. You will start to realize that those very things are your superpowers.

They make people feel seen.
They make you human.

And when you finally let go of trying to be perfect, you'll find peace. You'll laugh more. You'll sleep better. You'll start leading others, and you will live from a place of authenticity instead of approval.

You'll look back and see that the moments you thought were failures were actually turning points, and some of the greatest "non-resume" moments that made you who you are.

You'll look back and realize the people who challenged you were teachers.
And that the gratitude you learned along the way became your anchor.

So take a deep breath, younger me. You don't need to have it all figured out.

Just keep showing up, but show up more authentically even sooner. Be curious, kind, and real.

Pause—and think about what Maya Angelou said: "People will forget what you said, people will forget what you did, but people will never forget how you made them feel"

All my love!
Nadine

Nadine Lavigne
USA
https://www.linkedin.com/in/nadinelavigne/

Dear Lilly,

This is how I lead and love myself.

Every year, I set an intention.

Resolutions demand. Intentions guide.

I choose a single word-ish. I look up its definition, sit with it, and then define it for myself. It becomes the foundation I use to navigate the year ahead—a quiet compass for how I lead, love, and live.

My first word: Fearlessness.

Defined as "lack of fear." That felt impossible. So I made it mean "moving through fear anyway."
So that I can stop waiting for the absence of fear to start.

Then came Courage.

Defined as "mental or moral strength to persevere." For me, it became "acts small and large that honor truth." That year, I leaned in, and I also blew up my career and started again, this time on my own terms.

So that I can live without regret for what I didn't try.

Next was Breathe.

Defined as "to pause for rest."
After courage, I needed that one. It meant creating space to exhale, to reset, to listen again.

So that I can remember who I am beneath the noise.

Then came Do Less Better.

Defined as "focus on what truly matters."
It became a filter for my time, energy, and attention.
So that I can create excellence without exhaustion.

After that, Freedom.

Defined as "the power to act, speak, or think as one wants."
For me, it meant releasing attachment to outcomes and loosening my grip on how things should look.
So that I can make choices from alignment, not approval.

And this year: Truth.

Defined as "that which is in accordance with fact or reality."

It has become an invitation to live fully in integrity with who I am now.

So that I can lead with honesty and rest easy in my own skin.

Here's how I set my intention:

1. Look back with expansion.

   What gave you energy? What drained it? Three of each. Energy is data.

2. Name your year.

   One word. A compass, not a caption. Once you name it, your choices find their place.

3. Write a Stop-Doing list.

   The most loving document you'll ever create. Leadership begins with subtraction.

4. Calendar your courage.

   Intentions die in "someday." Put the brave things on actual dates.

5. Measure what matters.

   Moments, not metrics. Did I show up with honesty? With curiosity? That's the real ROI.

6. Rehearse forgiveness.

   You will wobble. You will forget. No drama. Just the truth.

And the most important: Invite company.
Share your word with two people who will walk with you.
Send tiny wins. "Said no." "Took the leap." "Chose truth."

Because leadership, like life, is a shared experiment. The way you live your word gives others permission to live theirs.

So choose yours. Define it. Make it your own. Add your "so that I can."
And remember, you don't need a new year to begin again.
You just need a new breath.

With love, grit, and a lot of courage,
Ricki

Ricki Pasinelli
USA
https://www.linkedin.com/in/ricki-pasinelli/

Dear Lilly,

Everyone has a background and a story that shapes how they show up—in business and in life. Yours will be no different. You'll carry the lessons of where you've been, the people who built you, and the moments that nearly broke you. Don't hide from any of it. Every chapter will teach you how to lead with both intellect and instinct, a balance that can't be imitated.

You'll learn, sometimes painfully, that passion isn't always enough. No matter how urgent the need or how clear the vision, timing is everything. Without alignment, even the best intentions can turn into chaos dressed up as strategy. You'll want to move fast—to fix, to build, to prove. But leadership isn't a race; it's a rhythm. Wait for alignment, and you'll move further with less resistance.

Respect, you'll find, is a form of currency—one that must be earned and guarded with care. It's what allows you to disagree without disconnecting, to challenge without wounding, and to lead without losing yourself. Offer it with intention, and it becomes the quiet force that carries your name further than any title ever will.

And then there's resilience; the part no one prepares you for. It will demand that you go through, stand in, and rise from pressures you never saw coming. There will be moments when silence will test your patience, when grace will feel like surrender, and when courage will cost you comfort. Choose it anyway. That's where strength finds its voice.

One day, you'll understand that leadership isn't measured by position or praise. It's proven in the still moments when clarity demands courage and integrity costs you comfort. Real leaders don't rise to be seen; they rise to make space for others to stand taller. That's where legacy lives.

Keep your heels grounded in respect, your head lifted in purpose, and your heart open enough to keep learning. You won't always get it right, but you'll always rise right.

And when you do—lead with truth, walk with grace, and leave the kind of imprint that reminds others: real leadership doesn't chase recognition. It builds legacies, through alignment, respect, and resilience.

(Anonymous)

Dear Lilly,

You grew up believing that to be "normal," you had to think in straight lines—logic over instinct, facts over feelings, order over flow—with every strand of hair coiffed perfectly in place. You learned (tried) to package your thoughts neatly, to move from point A to B without detouring through wonder or doubt. And for a while, that worked. It got you respect. It kept you safe.

But eventually you see that your mind was never meant to be kept on a leash. It loops and links, mapping patterns others miss, finding harmony in the cacophony of opinions and equities. What looks like distraction is often discovery. What feels like overthinking is sometimes insight trying to surface. You don't reach clarity by standing still, you find it through motion, through exchange, through engagement.

And when life strips away what once felt certain—when something you thought was permanent disappears overnight—you learn to listen differently. You start to notice what endures: the pulse beneath the noise, a quiet sense of knowing that doesn't need proof. You realize clarity isn't about control; it's about trust; the kind that lets you follow your own wild current, even when it pulls you off the map.

You'll also learn that being a good manager and being a good leader are not the same thing. Management keeps things running; leadership decides where to go next. And while some days you'll feel like you can't even manage yourself, you'll one day find yourself calmly steering multimillion-dollar programs with precision and confidence, building a community of champions along the way—because real leadership isn't about loving spreadsheets. It's about seeing systems clearly, translating complexity into clarity, and helping people move together toward something larger than themselves.

Stop sanding down your edges to fit into rooms that weren't built for how you think. Those edges are the reason you'll eventually be asked to redesign the room.

And when you finally stop apologizing for how your mind works, for being too effusive, too intense, too much, you'll see that your "weirdness" was never a flaw. It's creative intelligence in its raw form, reminding you of your power.

You were never meant to think like everyone else. You were meant to see differently and to make that vision real.

With love,
Anonymous

Dear Lilly,

Let me share with you some recent happy news which brought with it a realization of what home really means to me.

My baby sister got her British citizenship yesterday. And while I lovingly tease her that we are now both officially traitors to our birth country, my heart is full of pride seeing her thrive in her adopted country with grit, resilience and staying true to the values our parents taught us—always be brave no matter what life serves you, and above all, always be kind.

The ceremony brought back a realization I had when I visited The Philippines early this year. It was the first time I went home with both parents gone to the other side… our house now empty with a for sale sign on the wall. I spent precious time with loving aunts, uncles, nieces and nephews, and my old sweet childhood friends, all of whom knew me from when I was a young child up to the time when I became unapologetically ambitious and thought I owed it to the universe to get the most out of this life I was given.

After more than 3 decades in the Netherlands, I realized no matter how truly happy I am here (I found the love of my life, raised 2 wonderful happy human beings, am doing the work that I love where I can make use of the talents given to me), there will always be a part of me which is sorry to have missed so much time with my parents, family and friends. The lost times of shared laughter and tears with my loved ones in The Philippines are what I now have come to accept as my "trade-off". There is something uniquely special about being with people one shared history with as a child. There is this pure understanding and acceptance of one's little habits and even one's idiosyncrasies. There is no need for words of explanation somehow, because they know me and where I came from.

Don't get me wrong, I have real and warm connections here too, but no one will understand without me explaining why I like to buy books and never borrow from the library. My family in The Philippines all know I used to camp out in dark, musty libraries because I did not have money to buy my own books. They know I used to buy second hand ones on the streets of busy Manila during my college years just because I had this weird longing to have the books I love next to my bed at home. And weirdly enough, I still have some of those in my home here in the Netherlands. Those were the first things I packed in my luggage before I took off to Europe 30+ years ago.

And so I think being conscious and coming to peace with that trade-off is what makes the lives of immigrants like me and my sister more meaningful... because while we may have left our homeland for greener pastures, our hearts will remain connected to The Philippines, where loving memories with our family and friends will always remind us that no amount of distance nor time will keep us from calling The Philippines our home.

Sincerely,
Vina

Vina Westland-Magsino
The Netherlands
https://www.linkedin.com/in/vwestlandmagsino

Dear Lilly,

It's time to pack for another trip to Hong Kong. Spending two weeks 8,000 miles from home is always hard. It's hardest knowing you're missing milestones. Those FaceTime calls on the iPad feel like the only thing keeping you from sobbing, and the 13-hour time difference and packed agenda of meetings and dinners make even those a challenge. But you always make those calls happen, even if you feel like all eyes are on you when you excuse yourself from the table.

These trips aren't optional, and they're also rewarding: seeing places and experiencing cultures you never imagined, meeting the people you email every day, finally face to face. And you find small ways to stay connected: mailing dolls and surprises ahead of time so they appear at home while you're gone, and picking up little treasures from the Hong Kong Disney Store at the airport to tuck into your carryon for when you return. And you're able to do it because someone is home holding down the fort, reading Harry Potter to her and sparking her love of books, making sure she never feels the distance as much as you do.

As she gets older, your daughter returns the favor, making care package boxes for you to take with you containing notes, drawings, and your favorite candies.

Here's what you don't realize yet: you're not choosing work over being a good mom. You're showing her what leadership looks like. Not the travel or the titles, but the responsibility, the curiosity, and the ability to walk into unfamiliar places and hold your own.

And here's the lesson in loving yourself: you don't have to feel guilty for wanting a career that matters to you. You are allowed to be both ambitious and caring. One day, you'll see that your daughter didn't need what you perceived as perfection, she needed parents who loved her and wanted her to have everything. And that, she certainly had.

When you see the young woman she becomes, caring, thoughtful, smart, and already far more accomplished than you were at her age, you will know: You did better than you ever gave yourself credit for.

With love,
Melissa

Melissa Cohen
USA
https://www.linkedin.com/in/melissa-beth-cohen/

Dear Lilly,

I guess it's about time that I tell you why I decided to write all these letters to you.

As you have already read, you have had many lessons in your life, but none as impactful as the lesson you learned in 2023.

If you aren't already sitting down reading this, please do.

In 2023 you began having strokes. The first hospitalization was minor, but the second resulted in you losing your speech, sight in your right eye, the structure in the right side of your face, and the ability to move your or feel your right arm, hand, and fingers. With the emergency room machines blaring, your heart rate and blood pressure were rising. You were terrified, crying, unable to get your words out. And worse, you were unsure of whether you might… well…. die.

While the nurses and doctor were moving all over the room you had two specific thoughts: "But I am not done yet," and "But if I am, I'm so thankful for this amazing life that I have lived."

I know this is hard to read, and thankfully all those losses were temporary. However, the work required to identify the cause of those strokes after the hospitalizations was intense (a letter for another day).

What I need you to know now is that never, ever did you think this may be part of your journey. You had managed so much in your life, never could you imagine that it could all be over in your forties.

This event changes you forever.

You have always understood that life is precious, but now you also realize just how quickly everything can be taken from you. It makes you evaluate all of those moments that you said, "I will do that when…" (when I am not so tired, when work slows down, when I retire… the 'when' list is long).

My Dear Lilly, "when" may never come. You must enjoy every minute of your life. Every. Single. Day. There is so much more to this story that I will share with you, but for now, what I need you to know is that the doctors will get to the bottom of this (in time). You will become committed to those items on your bucket list, NOW—not when.

Shared Lesson in Leadership and Loving Yourself: Nothing is more important than your health. Nothing! If you aren't taking care of yourself, you can't take care of anything or anybody else. Not your family, your company, or your community.

Love Always,
Ali

We get one chance at this life. Please make sure to live it!